DORIE:
THE GIRL NOBODY LOVED

DORIE:
THE GIRL NOBODY LOVED

DORIS VAN STONE

with

ERWIN LUTZER

MOODY PRESS

CHICAGO

Library of Congress Cataloging in Publication Data
Van Stone, Doris.
  Dorie, the girl nobody loved.

  1. Van Stone, Doris. 2. Missionaries—New Guinea—
Biography. 3. Missionaries—United States—Biography.
I. Lutzer, Erwin, joint author. II. Title.
BV3680.N52V358   266'.023'0924 [B]   78-17935
         ISBN 0-8024-2275-6
     Moody Paperback Edition, 1981

       25 27 29 30 28 26 24

Printed in the United States of America

To
Burney and Darlene
who gave me
the privilege of being called
"Mother"

Contents

Foreword

I read with tears in my eyes this powerful story of the little girl nobody loved turning into the woman God chose and used. Humanly speaking, Dorie's childhood of unbelievably cruel treatment and total rejection should have produced an emotionally unstable, bitter adult. But instead, Christ, as her newfound Savior, rescued her and, little by little, transformed her into a well-adjusted adult.

I was moved by the way Dorie was miraculously sustained by her only material possession, a little New Testament, during her time of terrible aloneness in the world. She underlined, memorized, and clung to its promises. It was her only friend. But it proved to be sufficient.

This story shows beautifully how one can crawl out from under a self-image of complete ugliness not only into God's acceptance and love but also into a successful ministry for Him. It is a fantastic picture of Christ understanding and caring for and lifting up an unloved, beaten, and neglected child, and then healing her and miraculously preventing a permanent emotional scar.

But to me the most beautiful part of Dorie's life is that she is now using her childhood experiences to help other battered children work through their hurts, bringing them the same hope she found—Jesus.

EVELYN CHRISTENSON

1

Mother, Please Come Home

I walked quietly to the window and stared into the darkness. My eyes followed the headlights of each passing car. I sat on my brown wooden stool, my hands tucked under my legs, trying desperately to keep warm.

Hours passed. Finally I saw the shadowy form of my mother turn the corner and come up the walk. By the time she reached our second-floor apartment, I had groped through the dark room to meet her.

I hope she'll be glad to see me. But as usual she brushed past me and gathered my sister Marie* into a hug. "Honey, how are you?" she cooed. I stood, my hands stuffed in the pockets of my faded coveralls, waiting for her to love me. But she pushed me away. "What do you want?" she barked.

"Would you hug me?" I asked timidly.

"You get out of here!" she barked back.

I was only six. But scenes from that apartment are etched indelibly on my mind. I remember nothing bright. Dark woodwork trimmed the drab walls. A brown overstuffed chair, a bench, and a small rug furnished the front room. The next room was bare except for a bed, shared by Marie and me, that pulled down from the closet.

Each morning my mother left early and was gone until late at night. I can still see her—jet black hair framing her perfectly oval face. Her brown eyes turned stony as she

*This name has been changed.

11

shouted, "Doris, take good care of your sister. And remember, don't turn on the lights!"

Marie was a year younger than I, and my mother was anxious for me to understand one thing clearly: if anything happened to Marie, I would be blamed. The responsibility rested with me.

Marie and I spent our days in the apartment alone. We looked forward to the weekends when Mother would fix us something to eat. On those mornings she slept late, and then the three of us ate together in silence. But most of the time our menu consisted of the only food a six-year-old can fix: peanut-butter-and-jelly sandwiches. I could reach the jar in the pantry. Holding the jar between my knees, I twisted and scraped with a knife to mix the oil and peanut butter. "Don't spill the oil," Mother had warned. If I did, I quickly mopped it up with toilet paper. I spread the peanut butter, gouging holes in the bread. If we had no jelly, we gulped it down as best we could.

Occasionally we had milk, but usually we drank water. We had no tin tumblers, only jelly-jar glasses. Having been whipped for breaking one of them, I learned caution. I pulled a chair up to the porcelain sink set the glass under the spout, then turned on the water. With both hands, I passed the glass to Marie, then climbed down.

Our stomachs often growled with hunger. Once I bravely walked to the store, hoping the grocer would give me some food. When he said no, I promised that my mother would pay the next day. I learned that only people with money could have food. Reluctantly, I walked home to the apartment empty-handed—and hungry.

Each evening waiting for my mother, I felt alone, responsible. I was terrified that something awful would happen to me or my sister. The darkness of our dingy apartment fed my childish imagination. *What if Mother doesn't come home?*

One evening we heard the door open on the first floor of the apartment building. I grabbed a butcher knife from the kitchen, opened the door of our apartment, and saw two drunks standing at the bottom of the stairway. Clutching the knife till my knuckles turned white, I yelled, "Get out! I've got a knife!" with all the fierceness I could muster. Marie hid behind me. They laughed, then left a few moments later.

When I reported the terror to Mother, she shrugged. "So? They didn't come in, did they?" Then she asked the only question that mattered. "Did you have the lights on?"

That's why I put my chair next to the window. The car lights moving along 34th Street in Oakland, California, were more friendly than the haunting darkness of the cold apartment. I was afraid to fall asleep without Mother there. Sometimes Marie would cry out, terrified by strange noises. I would calmly put my arm around her shoulders, telling her not to worry. Inside I was terrified. Night after night I sat in the dark and worried about what Mother would do to me if Marie became sick or was hurt.

When Mother did arrive late in the evening she didn't speak to me but always quickly went to find Marie, who usually had fallen asleep on the couch. "Marie is a pretty girl—she's not like you," my mother would often say. She tucked Marie into bed and kissed her good night. I was on my own.

Without changing my clothes—I had no pajamas—I crawled under the covers next to my sister. Not once did my mother hug me or let me sit on her lap.

Occasionally, my mother would bring a gift for Marie, but never for me. Our clothes were given to us by our friends next door. Our dresses always seemed to be either too small or too big; our trousers were worn bare at the knee, and our shoes pinched our toes. Anything new was given to Marie.

When Mother was home I hid my fears. I would crawl behind a couch where I could sob undetected. Sometimes when my stomach ached, I sat doubled over on the floor. If Mother found me crying, she would spank me.

Late one evening I awoke and Marie was not in bed beside me. I called for Mother, who had come home earlier, but I received no answer. Frantically, I searched the four rooms of our dark apartment. Thinking I had been abandoned, I began to scream. I crouched in a corner crying hysterically. Perhaps an hour passed. Suddenly I heard someone on the stairs. Then I saw Mother at the door with Marie in her arms. She had left me without telling me, and she never explained her disappearance.

One afternoon my mother took Marie and me to visit a friend. Marie sat on my mother's lap while the woman admired my sister's beautiful features. Then, in a not too subtle reference to me, the woman added, "But it's too bad about the other one."

What is so different about me? Why am I so ugly? Can't anyone love me? Dejected, I slid off my chair and squatted in a corner. My emotions imprisoned me; no one spoke to me, and I did not care to speak. Even this woman regretted that I had been born.

Perhaps I can make Mother love me, I thought. But whenever I put my arm around her, she would push me away. If I tried to climb onto her lap, she would brush me aside like one might do to a friendly but unwanted dog. "Don't do that," she would snap. Then she would add, "And don't call me Mother. Call me Laura."

At the age of six I knew I was unwanted. A disgrace, a burden, a nuisance—I didn't know the meaning of those words, but I felt every ounce of their weight. *I'm ugly, and it's my fault. If only I could do something about it!*

The days dragged on hopelessly in dreary succession.

Marie and I seldom laughed. Mostly we just sat and wondered what was wrong in our world.

A few hundred feet from our apartment was an empty lot where my sister and I played. We had no toys, but used odd objects such as sticks or stones to represent anything our imaginations desired. There we would forget our fears, but not for long.

We sensed that other children had fun. They were happy and carefree, but we found it difficult to enjoy ourselves. Our fleeting fun times could not erase the hurt we knew so well. Something was wrong in our home. We found it hard to be friendly or smile.

My father came to the apartment perhaps three or four times. Although I recall little about him from those visits, I remember his saying how cute Marie was. She was his favorite, too.

One small shaft of light penetrates the dark memories of those days—the corner drugstore. I went as often as I dared. "Hi there, Clara Bow," the druggist would greet me, gracing me with a nickname. "Want a soda?"

I would say no, for I had no money. But his eyes twinkled with kindness as he lifted me onto a revolving stool and gave me a strawberry soda. *Please see beneath my shabby clothes and see how afraid I am. I hurt!* Although he couldn't see that deeply, he gave me my first experience of human love.

Those trips to the drugstore soon ended. My mother made a decision that radically affected our future.

Our days in the apartment were over.

2

The Orphanage

"Children, your father and I can't take care of you, so you're going to a home you'll enjoy," Mother told us as she and her friend loaded Marie and me onto a streetcar. We rode a while, then walked. Mother held our hands. I carried our few tattered clothes in a paper bag. We had no toys.

As we walked, I saw a large, gold-shingled building. Two-storied and U-shaped, it looked huge to me. A palm tree encircled by geraniums towered in the courtyard. Through a chain-link fence I saw some boys playing. *Must be a school,* I thought.

"Good-bye," Mother said without a tear. "I'll see you." She didn't say when.

Both of the women walked toward the door. The sadness on the neighbor lady's face reflected her concern for us. (I secretly hoped she would visit us sometime, but she never did.) Mother paused, her hand on the doorknob. "Maybe you won't have to stay here too long." Then the door closed, and we were left alone. It was as if Mother had dropped off a package and never remembered to come back and pick it up.

We had arrived just before lunch, so we were taken to a dining room where about sixty-five children sat at long tables.

"Doris," the matron said, "you'll learn that you do not talk at the table. If you want anything, raise your hand."

At that first meal we were served beets. "I don't like beets," I told the matron.

"You'll learn to like them," she informed me. "You won't be dismissed from the table until they're eaten." But I was determined that no beets would go down my throat. I sat and sat. But I didn't touch the beets. "Doris, eat your beets," the matron reminded. I didn't answer. But I didn't eat. Finally the other children were dismissed. I still sat. At midafternoon the matron took away my chair.

Eventually the other children came in for dinner. I was given nothing, since I had not eaten my beets. When the other children had finished dinner, they left. I sat until 9 P.M. Again they took away my chair. I stood, but I didn't eat the beets. I thought I was winning, but a matron soon came with a long, thin paddle and gave me a beating I'll never forget.

I was marched upstairs and shown the dressing room. Each child had a cubby hole called a clothes press with a hook for clothes and a shelf above for bath towels. Shoes were placed beneath. The other children were already in bed, so I dressed alone. The matron pointed out my cot, one of twenty lining the room. There were no rugs except a runner down the center aisle. It began to dawn on me that this was a strange school.

"Will my mother come back?" I asked.

"Oh, she'll come to see you," the matron said, giving no definite promise.

That first night I did something that I repeated every night for the next seven years: I cried myself to sleep.

After a few days I began to inquire of the other children. "What do you call this place?"

"It's an orphanage," they answered. "An orphanage." A big girl with dark hair told me solemnly, "This is a place you go when nobody wants you."

Our mother had not bothered to tour the orphanage. Miss Ward, a stout woman with gray hair and blue eyes, introduced us to the matron, Miss Gabriel. Miss Gabriel showed us the playroom, with toys to be shared by all the children. Along one wall was a long row of wooden boxes with lids for each child to store private possessions. Mine would be the first one in the corner. But I had nothing to put in my box.

Sometimes during playtime I would ask another child if I could keep a toy in my box. But she would say, "No. It's mine!" So I acquired some things of my own. If I found an unbroken crayon, I would slip it in my box when no one was looking. Or if I was coloring a picture, I would put it in my box so no one would mess it up.

I always stacked my things carefully so that, if necessary, I could leave in a hurry. *Mother said we might not have to stay too long. Perhaps we'll leave any minute,* I thought.

At first I was a loner. I spent my free time sitting on a long, green slat bench, rocking back and forth, wondering how I could get out. My feet dangled to the floor. I tucked my hands under my legs, just as I had done at the window of the apartment. *When will Mother return?*

How I wished I could be back in the familiar apartment. Children would ask me to play with them, but I refused. *I won't be here long,* I assured myself.

While living in the apartment, I had been given a red sweater with tan trim and wooden buttons. Now I wore it every day, buttoning my security around me. Miss Gabriel could scarcely persuade me to part with it on washdays. It was my only link with what I knew as home.

Days and weeks passed, and Mother did not return. Reluctantly I accepted the fact that she might not keep her promise. Apparently we were here to stay. In fact, I assumed Marie and I would be there the rest of our lives.

Slowly, I began to adjust to the routine. *If I can be*

tough, I can survive, I figured. I bullied the other children. I was never subtle. I pushed and shoved. I hit. If another child wouldn't let me see his toy, I would grab it. The others didn't hit me, but I hit them and felt good about it. I wasn't bigger or stronger than the others, but I must have looked tough.

The daily schedule was monotonous. The morning bell got us out of bed, and we lined up for breakfast. Every day we had mush—lumpy, sticky, cooked cereal. Taxing my ingenuity to the limit, I devised a plan to avoid swallowing the slime. First, I stuffed it in my mouth, making my fat cheeks fatter. Then I raised my hand to go to the bathroom, where I spit it in the sink. I did that every morning.

On one such trip to the bathroom, I felt the matron's strong hand on the nape of my neck. "Come here, Doris!" she commanded, causing every head in the dining room to turn in my direction. She marched me to the wash area, and I spit the mush into the sink, aiming it into the drain hole. Then she took a bar of soap and coated my tongue. The next day the mush tasted somewhat better. From then on I ate it.

Every Tuesday and Thursday we had buttermilk. I hated that white, curdly stuff, so I forced other girls to drink mine. Although they hated it too, they drank theirs quickly to get the ordeal over. When the matron was not looking, I would switch glasses. "If you don't drink it, I'll get you in the yard," I would threaten. My reputation for meanness made them wince and obey.

Marie and I did not often play together. She was assigned to another part of the building with the five-year-olds; I was with the six- to eight-year-olds. The orphanage would not tolerate close ties between members of the same family or even close friendships among the children. Later I learned the reason: in a close friendship if one child is adopted, the other is deeply hurt.

I became good friends with Esther, a friendly, blond girl whose bed was close to mine. Then, unexpectedly, she was gone; she had been adopted. The orphanage staff arranged her leave when all of us were in school to avoid the good-byes. That evening, when I realized Esther was gone, I flung myself across the narrow cot and wept bitterly. I knew I would never see her again. The matron had warned us, "Don't make close friendships, or you'll be hurt."

Miss Gabriel, whom we dubbed "Angel Gabriel" although she lacked virtually all angelic qualities, controlled us with the discipline of an army corporal. Her jet black hair was worn in a double bun, like a double-decker ice-cream cone. She had a hooked nose and coal black eyes. "I can see clean through you," she would assure us as she stared down at us without blinking. We believed her.

She believed strongly that sickness was always the result of sin, especially the sin of disobeying her orders. Whenever one of us was sick, she'd put the illness into theological perspective. "It's the Lord! He's punishing you!" she snapped. "If you weren't so naughty, you wouldn't be sick." We endured what we believed was the Lord's punishment, trying to figure out exactly what sin we had committed to deserve a cold, the flu, or even the sniffles. But one day Angel Gabriel received a crash course in theology: she came down with the mumps!

I got into trouble often enough for my misbehavior. But even if I was punished unjustly, the other girls were unsympathetic. I'd done enough mean things to deserve it. One morning, when we were lined up for instructions, one of the girls stuck out her tongue at Miss Gabriel. The Angel impulsively swung her arm in the direction of the girl's head. The girl ducked, and I was standing directly behind her. My face stung from the blow.

"But, Miss Gabriel, I didn't do it!" I wailed, louder than was necessary.

"I know, but you'll deserve it next week," Miss Gabriel assured me. She didn't apologize.

That night Miss Gabriel found me crying before I fell asleep. "Not you again, Doris," she muttered; and then she gave me a whipping. I learned to cry silently, my head tucked under the blankets.

The Angel also beat us for watching the athletes of the Oakland Technical High School work out next door. Why that was forbidden will have to remain one of life's imponderable mysteries.

When I got older, I took out my resentment against Miss Gabriel on the laundry. My job was to sort and hang the laundered dresses. Our dresses were heavily starched and pressed flat. That ruined any ruffles. The clothes were so stiff, in fact, that I had to ram a yardstick between the layers to separate them. When Miss Gabriel wasn't looking, I would talk to the clothes like she talked to us.

"Molly, one more word out of you and I'll send you out of the dining room," I'd say, mimicking the Angel's venom. Or, "Jeannie, eat that mush or I'll ram it down your throat."

Another job, when I was nine, was to help the little girls get dressed. One five-year-old always wet her bed. She'd deliberately sit on her bed and wet it. I had to change her sheets, and got disgusted. One morning after Miss Gabriel had gone, I took that little girl and rubbed her nose in the wet bed.

"Dorie!" the other girls gasped. But she never wet her bed again.

Although I had a reputation for being tough, I eventually wanted to play with the others. At first I hung at the outskirts, watching. "We don't want you," they would tell me. I had to learn to be friendly. "Please, can I play?" I'd beg. "I promise I won't hit you." As I learned not to be so mean, they included me.

In school, those of us from the orphanage could be easily identified by our shabby clothes and distinctive haircuts. On a specified day, a chair was put on a low table. One by one we would crawl onto the table, then perch on the chair. Miss Gabriel would place a bowl on our heads. The vessel was so huge it reminded me of an umbrella—we could have gone under it for shade: Then she would snip off our hair.

Posing with classmates at Emerson School in Oakland, where I attended while living at the orphanage. I am fifth from the right in the front row. (1932)

When we marched to school we'd all look alike. As cars passed, they would slow down. Parents pointed us out to their children. *We're all oddballs and besides, I'm ugly,* I thought.

Two interests preserved my sanity during those years. One was my love for books, and the second was my ability to draw. Not even Angel Gabriel could change my desire to read books. I would sneak into the parlor and look carefully at the long rows of books high on the shelves. There I would find *Huckleberry Finn, Tom Sawyer,* or *Black Beauty* and read them in snatches. Poring over their pages, I escaped into a world of pleasant experiences. I devoured *Heidi* and the *Pollyanna* series.

But my favorites were the *Mother West Wind* series. As I read about the little animals running free in the forest, I fantasized being as cute and adored as the squirrels and possums.

Sometimes the Angel caught me reading when I was to be working, or she found me reading at odd hours. However, the whippings I received could not deter me from those books, the only friends I could count on. They lifted me out of the monotonous and depressing world of the orphanage.

Also, I loved art. I'd look at a scene and sketch it with my left hand. The school, however, had a policy that all children must use their right hands. For me that was almost impossible. I wrote poorly and began stuttering. Try as I might, the words would come out of my mouth in pieces.

One day when the teacher wasn't looking, I sketched a picture of children on a hill flying a kite. "Doris, you didn't do this!" the teacher snapped when she walked past my desk.

"Yes—I di-id."

"No, you didn't!"

"Ye-es—I di-id."

She took a ruler and slapped me across the knuckles. Just then she caught the eye of the girl across the aisle. "Did Doris draw this?" she asked.

"Yes," the girl replied meekly.

"How did you do this, Doris?" she questioned, somewhat subdued.

"I di-id-n't do-do it with thi-is hand, but thi-is one," I stammered, pointing to my left hand.

With that, she snatched the picture and walked to the principal's office. Later that day the teacher told me some good news: the principal had granted permission for me to use my left hand!

It wasn't long before I began to enjoy school and eventually grew out of my speech impediment. At last I was beginning to be accepted for what I could do rather than for the way I looked.

As we grew older, the orphanage staff would give the children permission to go for long walks together. Every Saturday evening I would go directly to the corner drugstore to see *The Saturday Evening Post*, which usually had a drawing by Norman Rockwell on the cover. I would study it, analyze it, and envy it. I developed a secret ambition. *Someday my drawings will be there,* I mused.

I would wait until dusk to take my walk, then would go as close to the houses as I dared. I'd see the children playing together on the floor, or the family eating together. I'd see the mother cooking. I could not imagine what that would be like.

When I returned to the orphanage, I dreamed of living on the outside, where no one would scold me, and where I could have all I wanted to eat. I could talk as much as I liked, and no one would tell me to be quiet. I could have clean sheets every night and could change my clothes twice a day if I wanted.

Sometimes when the matron was sleeping, I would sneak out of my bed and tiptoe into the hallway and stand in front of the long mirror in our communal dressing room. I'd take my steel comb, let a few drops of water from the faucet fall on it, and change my hair style. First, I parted my hair on the left side, then on the right, and finally down the middle. At last, I'd brush it straight back. My kinky black hair simply would not fix. The stubborn curls clung close to my scalp. I envied other girls who could actually change their hairdos; I was stuck with a crop of fuzzy black hair.

Since those adjustments didn't seem to improve my appearance, I worked on my facial expressions. Forcing a smile, I watched myself carefully—mouth closed, mouth open, teeth showing, teeth hidden. After I tried all the combinations I could think of, I climbed back into bed to cry myself to sleep once more.

3

In Search of Love

My mother had promised that she would visit us in the orphanage, and she did—twice in seven years. Upon that first visit I instinctively ran to her. "Mother! Mother!" I shouted, forgetting her instructions to call her "Laura." She pushed me aside, opened a shopping bag, and gave Marie a gift. Nothing had changed.

The word *father* meant little to me; my recollection of my father was distant and confused. When other children talked about their fathers, I shrugged it off. But I could not detach myself from the feelings I had for Laura. I clung to the hope that someday she would love me.

During the Christmas season I especially hoped that Mother would surprise us with a visit. Christmas in the orphanage may have seemed bleak to observers, but to me it was special. I'd never before celebrated Christmas. Each year we received the same gifts: dark brown stockings with garters, an orange or apple, and a candy cane. A large tree was placed in the corner of the parlor and decked with lights and baubles. We would sing carols.

Then there was the Christmas pageant. The story we portrayed was as predictable as the gifts: a ragged girl was pleasantly surprised by Santa Claus, who always brought her what she wanted. We all wondered why he never did the same for us. We had no idea of the real message of Christmas. Santa Claus, a dimly lit tree, and a pageant were the extent of our understanding of this holiday. God was only a word to us—a word that was breathed when grown-ups became angry.

The parents were invited to the program. Some came and even took their children home for Christmas. But our mother never showed. No greeting card, no gifts, no visit. Nothing. One child whose parents visited her taunted the rest of us, "My folks love me, but yours don't." I turned away, tears blinding my eyes. *Somebody, please love me!*

After I arrived at the orphanage, there was one event I eagerly anticipated. The children would talk about it with uninhibited glee. Once a month parents would come to the orphanage to inspect the children—just in case they would see one they wanted.

Our conversations would always be at a high pitch as the day approached. What would it be like to live in a foster home? Would we have our own rooms, new clothes, and a modern hair style? We visualized what freedom would mean; perhaps we could be like the other children in school. And maybe—just maybe—we'd even be adopted and have a permanent family. Our imaginations went wild; we were bug-eyed with excitement.

On the specified day we all entered a large room. Our shoes were shined, our faces were washed, and our hair was brushed. We stood in line, trying desperately to be on our best behavior. *Someone is going to love me today!*

The parents came in. They were well dressed and carefully manicured. We could hear their muffled conversations, "She's cute, isn't she?" or, "There's one we might want to talk about." My heart beat faster. *Try me,* I screamed within, hoping that someone would look at me and want me.

But my day never came. June was chosen; then Betty, Lily, and Joan, but not me. Virginia was excited as she packed her clothes to go to her new home. How I envied her! *If only someone would take me!*

Sometimes I would see a nice-looking lady and fantasize that she would choose me and make me beautiful. *Here I am; try me! I'll make a good daughter for you.* But I soon got the message. Only cute children were chosen.

I figured there must be a reason I was so terribly rejected. I decided I must be the ugliest child that ever walked. I felt so ugly on the inside that I believed I was ugly on the outside. I'd analyze each feature. *Maybe it's my curly hair or my nose.* Everyone else had a button nose. Mine just jutted out. Maybe it was my color. I was more olive skinned than the others. And I was chubby—downright fat.

Marie was everything I wanted to be. Like me, she had brown eyes, but I thought hers were beautiful. She, too, had dark hair, but hers lay in place. Her skin was fairer than mine. She was much thinner and had an oval face like Mother's instead of a round one like mine.

Sometimes I would stare at her until she'd say, "Would you quit looking at me like that!" I was looking for a way to be like her, but there was no way.

My dread of those "special days" escalated month by month. No doubt I reflected the rejection I felt. I must have sulked. My shoulders drooped with the agony of that lineup. I could not look up with smiling anticipation as the cute children did.

I detested being inspected by people I knew would never accept me, so I would hide. Miss Gabriel would send someone to find me, and I would be dragged into the room with a dirty, tear-stained face. And, of course, no one would want a girl who looked naughty.

Just before my thirteenth birthday a group of students from the University of California visited the orphanage. They invited us to sit on the floor to hear a Bible story. Our curiosity was aroused.

I cautiously sat in the back row, not knowing what to expect. They taught us a few short choruses and told us a

Bible story. "Jesus Christ died on the cross for you, and God loves you," one girl told us.

That's a lie! She's wrong! Nobody *loves me!* I felt like screaming. Maybe God did love someone, somewhere, but He obviously didn't care about me.

The student concluded, "If you want to accept God's love, please come forward and talk to us."

No one stirred. The floor was crowded with the seated children. For a fleeting moment I thought I might carefully choose my steps and walk to the front, but I didn't dare. Some of the children whom I had mistreated were directly in front of me. If I had walked to the front, no doubt someone would have tried to trip me.

The students gathered their materials, preparing to leave. As they walked out the door one of them turned around and spoke slowly, "Children, even if you forget everything we have told you, remember—*God loves you.*" She spoke with such sincerity that I was stunned. I grabbed hold of that love. In my heart I knew it was true. I had no words to explain, but I knew He loved me.

Some of the children were already standing to leave, but I remained seated and took the risk of talking to God. *They said You love me. Nobody else does. If You want me, You can have me!* Instantly I felt that God was beside me, *in* me, in fact. An unexpected peace settled over me. *This must be God!*

That night in bed I cried for joy—I had found Somebody who loved me. "Oh, Doris, why are you crying again?" Angel Gabriel asked in obvious disgust. How could she understand? For the first time in my life I knew Somebody cared. I got spanked that evening for crying, but it didn't hurt like it once did. I had found a Friend.

A few weeks later a friendly matron, Irma Fremm, joined the orphanage staff. "Dorie, how'd you like to go to church with me?" she asked one Sunday morning.

"Go to church? I'd love to!" The orphanage staff gave me permission to attend the Gospel Tabernacle in Oakland with her. Miss Fremm encouraged me in the decision I had made to accept God's love. And there at the Gospel Tabernacle I was introduced for the first time to other Christians. I understood little of what was going on in the services; the songs were strange, the sermons above my head. But slowly I began to piece together what had happened that day in the orphanage: I had been accepted by God because of what Christ had done by dying on the cross for me. Someone had loved me enough to die for me! God loved me as I was, no matter how I looked.

One day Miss Fremm called, "Dorie, I have a gift for you." In her hand she carried a little package. Carefully, I unwrapped it, too excited to speak. It was a small black book, and on it was stamped, *The New Testament*. Tears blinded my eyes. This was the first gift I could remember receiving. It was the Bible, a book that I was told would help me understand my relationship with the God who loved me.

Several months after my thirteenth birthday, Marie and I had to leave the orphanage. The orphanage was equipped for children up to the age of twelve; after that we were sent to foster homes. My sister had lived in a foster home for a short time, but later was returned to the orphanage. I was glad when she came back; I still felt a responsibility to take care of her. I was relieved to discover that we would be leaving the orphanage together.

I worried, though, about how we would survive. People on the outside worked to earn money. Who would teach me to work? At the orphanage, Miss Gabriel chose our clothes each day. Although I never had more than three dresses, the choice of which to wear was never mine. *Would I know how to choose? Would I look right?*

Marie was reluctant to leave, but the next chapter in our

lives had already been planned. Apprehensively, we said good-bye to our friends at the orphanage. We were going out to live in the real world. We would soon discover that our days in the orphanage were happy—indeed, pleasant in comparison to the nightmare that would soon begin.

No longer could we be sure that we would have food to eat or clothes to wear. The orphanage, Miss Gabriel notwithstanding, had given us a sense of security, and we felt we belonged. Now we were on our own.

4

Mother, Where Are You?

I recall her face: deep wrinkles, gray eyes, a perpetual scowl, and short, gray hair. She was tall and about sixty-five. We called her "Granny." Marie and I were taken to her home, where we would adjust to the world outside of the orphanage.

We arrived at Granny's home in the fall, so I began to attend the Woodrow Wilson Junior High School in Oakland. Marie went to an elementary school nearby.

We were not told why Granny was given legal custody of us, but later it became obvious that this woman knew our mother. The day after our arrival we were initiated. "If you don't mind me, you'll get *this*—" she warned as she slapped us across the face with her bare hand. The blows stung, but Marie and I tried not to cry.

At mealtimes we were not permitted to eat at the table. We were expected to survive on leftovers. Too scared to complain, we tried to accept the situation as it was.

"You're just lucky to be here. You'd be out on the street if it wasn't for us," she shouted, sprinkling her sentences with generous doses of profanity. Her placid husband ignored us and helplessly tolerated his belligerent wife.

When she sent us to the grocery store, she would not allow us to make a list. Milk, bread, a head of lettuce, a can of peas—she continued rattling enough items to fill two bags. If we forgot an item, she would beat our legs with a mop handle.

My mother's warning to take care of Marie still stuck with me. Once when Granny threatened to beat Marie I stood between them. "Please beat me instead," I insisted. Granny thought that was a good idea.

How I thanked God for the five-mile walk to school each day. I had no close friends; I was afraid to speak to the other children lest they ask me questions about my parents or the family I lived with. But walking in the fresh air I talked out loud to God. "You've got to help me. Nobody else cares. Please, God, please!"·

One day Granny gave us a solemn command: "Go find your mother and ask her to give me money. If not, I'm going to get rid of you and your sister."

"But I don't know where she is," I protested.

"Go find her—just find her and get some money. And *don't bother coming back unless you do!*"

"But how will we find her?" I pleaded.

"I don't care, that's up to you." And with that Granny turned and walked away.

Marie and I left to begin searching the busy streets of Oakland for our mother. We knew only that she was a waitress somewhere. Granny's words rang in our ears: *come back with money or I'll get rid of you.*

We began searching the business section of Oakland, walking from restaurant to restaurant. Marie would stand in the doorway while I ventured inside as far as I dared, to look at the waitresses. Hour after hour we searched. Panic drove us on.

The menus in the windows and the scent of delicious food intensified our gnawing hunger. *If we could just sit down and eat!* We had no coats or sweaters. As the sun was setting we began to shiver. Marie started to cry. Yet we knew we could not return home empty-handed.

Lord, help us find her, I prayed, trying not to cry. The next restaurant was dingy, as dark inside as the dimly lit streets. Again Marie stood at the entrance. Pushing my way through the door, I dodged patrons who were making their exit. My eye caught the attention of a man wearing a white chef's hat. "I'm looking for my mother, sir. She's a waitress."

"We don't have anyone here with children," was the curt reply.

But across the room, writing an order, was Mother. With my eyes glued to her, I called across the aisle, "Mother!"

"I'm not your mother!" she snapped.

Then moving away from the tables and out of earshot, she hissed, "I'm going to tell the manager you are my sister. Now what do you want, anyway?"

"We need money."

"Well, I don't have any!"

"But Granny said she'd get rid of us, if—"

"Just tell her I don't have any," she interrupted. With that she turned to leave.

Unbelievingly, Marie and I left the restaurant. As we walked through the door onto the dark street, the tears came. *God, why did You disappoint us? You led us to the right restaurant. We found Mother with Your help—and now look what has happened!* Mother had publicly disowned us. We stood before her shivering, but she had shown no pity for our plight. We walked back to Granny's house empty-handed.

Granny was waiting with a stick. She beat me angrily, swearing at me for not bringing money. Then she shook me violently and grabbed my throat to choke me. Gasping for breath, I pleaded with her to stop. Marie became hysterical, "Doris will die. She'll die! Let her go!"

"Get out of the room," Granny screamed at her.

She tightened her hold on me. "I ought to choke you to death. That would make your mother happy, and we'd not have to worry about money," she shouted, shaking and choking me once more. Then she put me into a closet and locked the door.

"Stay there and think about what's happened. And the next time I tell you to do something, don't come home unless it's done!"

Hours later I was allowed to go to bed. For the first time, I contemplated running away. *Where shall I go, Lord?* I begged for an answer. Marie was twelve; I was thirteen, and we were under the legal custody of this woman. We had nowhere to go, so we had to stay.

I knew little about God, whom I had come to love only months before. But I knew that He cared. Whenever life became unbearable, as it often did, He would always provide a way of escape. Somehow, somewhere, He would help us, I was sure. Each day I would read the New Testament Irma Fremm had given me. Much of it was confusing, but I memorized some of the verses that were underlined: "I will never leave thee, nor forsake thee. So that we may boldly say, The Lord is my helper, and I will not fear what man shall do unto me" (Hebrews 13:5b-6). "Let not your heart be troubled: ye believe in God, believe also in me" (John 14:1).

Less than a week after the fruitless encounter with our mother, we returned home from school to find another woman at the house. She told us that our belongings were already in her car and that she was going to take us somewhere else to live. Granny had kept her word. We hadn't brought her the money; we had to leave. There was nothing to lose. In bewilderment we said good-bye to Granny.

It was a short drive, about three miles. We pulled up to a large stucco house with a neatly manicured lawn and play area. A group of girls was walking casually along the sidewalk as we took the box of clothes out of the car. Later we learned that this house was for girls who were wards of the court. Most of them were older than we, but living with them was a welcome respite from the cruelty of the past few months.

Here for the first time I shared what I knew about the love of Christ. I explained to the other girls that He could forgive our sin and bring us to God. Some seemed interested and asked me some pointed questions that I found hard to answer. One embittered girl, sensing my relatively cheerful attitude, lashed out at me, "Don't you realize that nobody cares about you?"

"Yes, I do. But Christ cares."

"What good is that? He's not helping you." Her voice trailed off as she walked away. But I was still convinced that my faith in God had done a lot of good. I knew that I too would have been bitter without the assurance that He loved me.

The food at the home was delicious—at least Marie and I thought so! For the first time my bed had a bedspread, and each of us had a separate dresser drawer. We had never known such luxury. Fortunately, I was able to continue going to school at Woodrow Wilson Junior High. This home was a haven; I hoped I would never have to leave.

But within four months we were told that Marie and I would be transferred to a private home. We greeted the news with excitement. *Maybe at last I'll find somebody who loves me.* We packed our belongings in boxes and waited for the car to pull up and take us to our new family.

5

Lord, It Hurts Too Much

The doorbell at the girls' home rang. I walked across the room to open the huge door. I was stunned. There stood Granny, looking as angry as ever. *Are we going back to her house?* I shuddered. With her was a woman we had never met.

"We've come to take you to a family that lives in San Francisco."

I was relieved. "Tell us more about them—who are they?"

"Their name is Makin. They know your mother."

That was not encouraging news. We got into the car and drove to the ferry for our ride across the bay. The ferry docked, and in a few moments the car stopped in front of a dark, shabby house.

Mr. and Mrs. Makin greeted us at the door. A short, stocky man with black hair, a five-o'clock shadow, and a heavy chest, he reminded me of a gorilla. Mrs. Makin seemed mousey-sallow complexion, and gray hair parted down the middle. They had a son, fifteen, and a daughter Susan, twelve—almost Marie's age. They were glad we had come to live with them; now Marie and I would do all the chores.

Less than eight months had passed since Marie and I had left the orphanage. We had spent about four months with Granny and perhaps four months at the girls' home. My fourteenth birthday was just around the corner; Marie was

was still twelve. Our move to San Francisco necessitated that we both attend the John Sweet Junior High School.

The day we arrived at the Makins I was told that I could not eat at the table with the family. This family knew my mother all right—Marie was permitted to eat with them. Furthermore, I could eat only if there were leftovers; if there were none, I would go hungry.

Their most popular dinner was fish. After the family was finished, I had the leftovers as promised. Mrs. Makin would take the head and the tail (sometimes if I was lucky there would be two heads and two tails), throw them into a pot of boiling powdered milk, and that was my meal.

How I loathed that beady fish-eye staring at me! It reminded me of Miss Gabriel, whose beady eyes could see through us. To this day, although I eat fish, I despise the sight of a fish baked *en toto*. Those eyes elicit memories I have long since tried to bury.

Marie spent most of her time playing with Susan. I dusted, washed clothes, chopped wood, and scrubbed the floor.

But worse than the fish heads and hard work were the undeserved beatings I regularly received. The Makins would argue, cursing and swearing, and then they'd take their anger out on me. They never beat Marie or their children. But they beat me mercilessly.

Often I'd hide in the Makins' walk-in closet and cry my eyes out. Other times I would ask Marie, "Why are they doing this to me?"

"I don't know," she would reply. Did she care about me? I don't know. But even if she did, she did not dare affiliate with me, or she would risk receiving the same treatment I got. Marie and I never discussed our cruel environment or analyzed reasons for our rejection. This was the way our life had always been. We knew nothing else.

I wanted desperately to be loved. Maybe I tried too hard.

When I would finish the dishes or the laundry, I would long for someone to say, "Dorie, you did a fine job." *What do I have to do to get people to say thank you?* I tried hard to please, but nothing worked.

I received no money for my work. Whenever I got a chance to baby-sit for the neighbors, the Makins would take the money from me. "It's for your keep," they would say.

Marie and I stood in line to receive our clothes from the Workers Project Administration, a program established by President Roosevelt during the Depression. We walked home carrying our precious cargo: baggy trousers, odd undergarments, and oversized boots.

My rollaway bed was in the hallway that led from the dining room to the Makins' bedroom. Marie slept with Susan. Frequently, strange men would walk past my couch, shuffling their way into my hostess's bedroom. One night a man stopped beside me, and pulled the covers off to embarrass me. I kicked and screamed; he left.

Though no one had taught me about sexual purity, I knew intuitively that sexual relationships apart from marriage were sin. *Lord, keep me pure.*

In retrospect, I believe that the Makins actually hoped I would succumb to some vice. Their hatred for me and affection for Marie led me to conclude that they would have welcomed a reason to get rid of me.

Mother visited us twice at the Makins. Despite the deep emotional wounds of the past, I was delighted to see her. "Mother!" I shouted.

"Don't call me 'Mother.' Call me 'Laura.' I didn't come to see you. Where's Marie? I have a gift for her."

A sharp pain cut through my body. I turned away, bitter and angry. That day I began to realize that she never would love me. By now I was old enough to understand why she rejected me so vehemently. By subtracting my age from my mother's, I knew she had been only fifteen when I was born. And although she never talked about it, I suspected that pregnancy forced her into an early marriage.

Knowing that did not dissolve my bitterness or erase my craving to be loved. I knew nowhere to turn, so again and again I turned to God. Every morning before I left for school, I would go into the bathroom, lock the door, and kneel beside the white bathtub. I took out the New Testament I had hidden in my purse and read it. I had to hide it or they would have taken it from me.

My Bible was like a book of love letters, a secret between me and the Lord. No one told me to memorize it. But as it spoke to me, I wanted to remember the words. I marked special verses, often placing a date beside them. Then I asked God to help me that day at school. I wouldn't have thought of starting a day without praying in that bathroom. Whatever the cruelties, I had one Friend—God.

Often when I came home I was afraid to go into the house, knowing that I probably would be whipped. So I would walk to a dark alley near the house and sleep on the cold concrete. That was more tolerable than the beatings I received at the Makins' front door.

Sometimes God spoke to me almost audibly. I'd be walking along the streets of San Francisco and see the beautifully dressed mannequins in the store windows. *Oh, if only I could have one new dress—*

I would hear the Lord say, "Dorie, you are beautifully clothed, not with garments that can be seen with human eyes, but with the righteousness of Christ."

I might be craving a decent meal. As I walked past restaurants and pastry shops, my hunger pangs were unbearable. Sometimes I even contemplated stealing. But the Lord would remind me, "Man shall not live by bread alone—"

In stores I would see husbands and wives walking arm in

arm. Or maybe they would be cuddling their children. *Lord, if I just had somebody to hold my hand!*

The Lord would say, "Dorie, I'll be your father and your mother, your brother and your sister. I will be with you; I even indwell you." Thankfully, God did not forsake me.

Periods of depression settled over me for days at a time. Repeatedly, I wondered if I would ever be free from the pain and emotional trauma that surged through my body.

Although the Makins had few luxuries, they had a floor-model radio near the front window. It was used only for special programs, and never to be used by me. But one Sunday afternoon when they were gone, I turned it on and accidentally found Charles E. Fuller and "The Old-Fashioned Revival Hour." My starving soul craved the warm music and message. Each Sunday afternoon I would pray that they would leave so I could glue my ears to the radio.

One Sunday I quietly left the house and began walking the streets, looking for a church where I could learn more about God and find someone who cared. I arbitrarily chose a large church on a corner, walked in, and sat near the back. The minister was giving a book report that morning. *This doesn't seem right,* I told myself on the way home.

The next Sunday I found a different church where the minister seemed to be saying the same things I had learned back in Oakland. Intuitively I knew that this man understood what I knew: God is real and we can depend upon His love.

After the service I introduced myself to the pastor, Dr. Lewis Jullianell. I discovered I was in the First Baptist Church of San Francisco. A few weeks later I shared bits and pieces of my story, fearing to tell all lest the Makins find out. Dr. Jullianell showed compassion, and to encourage me let me read the Scriptures in church. Other members invited me to public meetings in San Francisco's

Union Square. My confidence in sharing the gospel was developing. There at the First Baptist Church I was publicly identified with all believers; I was baptized.

Sometimes, to keep me from going to church, the Makins would say I first had to cut enough wood for their wood-burning stove. Although they gave me an impossibly high pile of logs, I swung the ax with all my might and finished. I would do anything to go to church.

At school I tried to be friendly, but I never made a close friend. I already knew I was different. The less people knew about my strange home, the better.

"Dorie, did that come out of the ark?" one student jibed, pointing to my torn dress. The others laughed. I forced a smile. All the other teenagers looked like teenagers—bobby socks, saddle shoes, bulky sweaters. How often I wished I could have spent the day in the rest room.

I had no lunch or lunch money. But I didn't want anyone to know. So every lunch period I went walking. If I had stayed, the sight of food would have been too much. Occasionally someone would offer me a sandwich. But I always said, "No thanks. I'm going for a walk." I stayed aloof, guarding my secret.

Often I tried to doctor my bleeding nose or touch up my black eye to appear presentable. When asked about my bruises, I lied. Plenty of excuses were available. I'd nonchalantly admit to being in a fight or other innocuous mischief. I was afraid that if the truth became known, the beatings would become more severe. I was gripped by fear. I had to survive.

At first, I made good grades. But after I had been nearly two years at the Makins, my grades began to slip. One of my teachers suspected that my low grades and shabby appearance were symptoms of home disturbances. I thank God for a teacher who took an interest in me.

One afternoon two juvenile authorities stopped me at

the school gate. "Are you Doris Duckworth?" one of them asked.

"Yes," I stammered. I froze in my tracks.

"Don't be afraid," the man assured me. He then handed me a piece of paper. "This is a summons for you to appear in juvenile court."

My fear subsided momentarily, but he added, "We have also informed the people you live with that your situation will be investigated. They will not have to go to court with you. But your mother will be charged with child negligence."

Numbly and slowly I walked home. I was scared. *Oh boy, now they know.* At first I wasn't going to return. But then I was afraid they would send someone to find me. Maybe even to kill me.

When I arrived, the Makins were waiting, their faces white with anger. "You get in here," Mr. Makin growled. He lumbered like a gorilla into the dining room. "Come in here."

My stomach tensed, but I went. Mrs. Makin followed me and stood in the narrow doorway. Feet apart and arms folded, she glared with fury.

"Get down on your knees," Mr. Makin said in his roughest voice. I obeyed, but I did not understand what was happening until he began unbuckling his belt. "The juvenile authorities have been here," he bellowed. He began beating me; the belt buckle gouged my back. Throbs of pain shot through my body.

Lord, this is too much!

"How could you do this to us?" Mr. Makin yelled, continuing to belt me. "We've given you a home. We've done you good. And you reported us to the police! That'll teach you to be grateful." His buckle landed on my neck. I clawed at the rug and screamed, terrified that I might be beaten to death.

I began looking for a way out. I couldn't go through the doorway; Mrs. Makin blocked it. But a plate glass window on the other side of the room extended almost to the floor. *Lord, if you'll help me—* I jumped, crashing through the glass and landing on my knees. My long-sleeved blouse protected my arms, so I escaped with only minor cuts.

I ran aimlessly into the semidarkness. Up and down the hills of San Francisco I ran, pausing every few minutes to catch my breath. Two and a half hours later I arrived at Fisherman's Wharf. My mind was reeling, my emotions were churning, and my body was aching from the beating and cuts. Sitting on the wharf, my feet dangling above the Pacific, I tried to put my thoughts together, piece by piece.

In the distance I saw the Golden Gate Bridge. A freighter moved slowly beneath it, pushing out to sea. How I wished I could take a slow boat to China.

But, of course, I could not take a boat anywhere that night. I longed for somewhere to go. *Lord, if only I could find a peaceful room where I could spend the night.* But I was alone with nowhere to go. Although I was fifteen, I was afraid to run away. If I were found I would be brought into court—or worse, maybe the Makins would kill me!

I dried my tears and wearily began the long walk back, bracing myself for the inevitable. Predictably, I was beaten again. In bed I sobbed and threw myself at God. Even then I did not doubt His love. Intuitively, I knew that He cared and that soon He would get me out of this mess. I always believed that He would not lay any burden on me that I couldn't bear. He would screen the trial, whittling it down to make it bearable. Even the beating seemed to hurt less when I remembered God was with me. But this night I was desperate. *Lord, I know You love me, but this is too much. Could You get me out of this place? Please!*

6

Woman, Is This Your Daughter?

By the time the court date arrived I was terrified. No one had explained to me what would happen; for all I knew the Makins might have been negotiating behind the scenes to put me in jail. My information consisted of a white piece of paper: I was to appear in court on a specified day at 10:00 A.M. Marie was not requested to join me.

At the door of the courthouse a woman kindly assured me that the court was sympathetic to my situation. The only purpose of the trial was to charge my mother with child neglect.

As I walked into the courtroom I glanced around, expecting to see my mother. But she was not there. *What if she doesn't come?* I wondered.

We waited silently for the judge to be seated. In a few moments he looked up, gazing solemnly at the small group gathered before him. "Doris Duckworth," he called. My heart sank.

The woman whom I had met moments before stepped to my side. "It's OK. Don't be afraid," she whispered as we walked to the front to stand before the judge.

"Laura Duckworth," the judged entoned. I heard my mother's footsteps behind me. Presently she was standing to my left. "Is this your daughter?" the judge asked.

There was a long pause—so long that I wondered if she might deny my identity. I raised my head slightly and caught the profile of her face through the corner of my eye.

"Yes, I suppose. But judge, I'd have gotten rid of her before she was born if I could have!"

A brief discussion followed. Then the judge ordered that Marie and I be permanently taken away from our mother. From now on we would be under the supervision of the courts. Wisely, the judge also ordered that I would be taken from the Makins and put in a new home.

O God, thank You for this, I silently prayed.

As we left the courtroom my mother turned to me and muttered, "If I ever see you again, I'll kill you!"

If ever I felt like I wanted to die, it was then. All hope was quenched. Her rejection of me was total and final. A heavy darkness engulfed me. *Am I that awful?* As I walked home alone, I prayed aloud that God would help me to understand why my mother abandoned me. I prayed that I wouldn't hate her. Hurt ripped through me as I tried to review my childhood, looking for something I'd done wrong. But I could find nothing.

Then I realized that my mother had never known love and did not know how to love. In that moment God let me forgive her. Tears flooded my eyes, and I felt sorry for her.

The hurt still wrenched deeply. But I had no hatred. The Lord let me know that He had been alone, too. They said all manner of evil against Him. And I was one of His followers. That day He performed a healing work in my life, and prevented a permanent scar.

The Makins had informed the court that they were willing to keep Marie as long as they got paid for her room and board. So she remained with them while I was transferred to a new home. Roy Milen of the First Baptist Church made arrangements to have me placed into the home of a church family.

My new guardians shook my hand as I entered their home. They were polite and kind, but they never gave me the warm hugs and acceptance I craved. I think they took me out of duty, not love. I was allowed to eat at the table, and they didn't yell at me or beat me. But though I tried desperately to please them, I could never get close. When my duties were done, I sat in my room alone. I never went into the family room unless invited.

I'm sure the people at church admired them for doing such a Christian deed. Yet they never gave me the warmth and fellowship necessary for survival. *This may be a Christian home,* I thought, *but it's not the kind I want.*

The wife was always suspicious, bent on believing the worst. One Sunday the offering disappeared. She accused me of stealing. When I said I hadn't stolen, she accused me of lying. Her criterion for judging guilt or innocence was simple: if I cried I was guilty; if my eyes were dry I was innocent. *Lord, don't let me cry!*

The one advantage of living with this family was that I could attend church regularly. There at the First Baptist Church I heard Robert G. Lee and Gypsy Smith. I absorbed all the knowledge I could, taking notes in almost every service.

One Wednesday while I was in prayer meeting, a man tapped me on the shoulder. He told me that a frantic woman was standing outside the church asking for her daughter, Doris. Fearfully, I walked outside, thinking that a tragedy had occurred. There was Laura: haggard, intoxicated, angry. She got to her story immediately. She had recently remarried (the fourth man since my father) and was concerned that her new husband not find out about Marie and me. She ranted and threatened suicide. Of course, I promised we wouldn't say anything. Indeed, I didn't even know where she was living, nor did I want to find out. I assured her that Marie and I would not expose her and that her new husband would never find out about us. She could return to him in peace. What a pitiful sight she was as she walked away from me. I couldn't hate her; I could only feel sorry.

Several months later Laura and I met unexpectedly on a street in Oakland. She was cuddling a new baby girl in her arms. My mother exclaimed, "Just look, isn't she a doll!" In her arms she held an adorable dark-haired girl. *Why, oh why could she not have loved me like that? What had I done to deserve her hatred and rejection?*

I had accepted the fact that my mother would never love me, but meeting her brought my wounded emotions to the surface again. I was not bitter toward her; God had helped me understand that bitterness would only contaminate me; it would never change her. But although the bitterness was past, the hurt was not. I longed for real love, not for the sympathy people in the church had so readily bestowed.

Marie and I kept in touch by seeing each other at the John Sweet Junior High School. One afternoon we met in the school yard. "Doris—" She hesitated, looking down. "I'm going to get married."

"Oh, no! Marie! You are scarcely fifteen, you can't—"

"Doris, you don't understand—"

"Please, Marie, please. You've got to finish school first, and then we'll work awhile and—"

"Doris, I'm going to have a *baby!*"

There on the playground a part of me died. My sister for whom I had felt responsible all those years was now being forced into an early marriage. I was dumbfounded.

The thought that something like *this* would happen had never crossed my mind. I had met her boyfriend once or twice when I was at the Makins. He was tall, perhaps seventeen or eighteen. Now my sister was pregnant. Soon she would be a mother. It all seemed so unfair. Marie had always had more advantages than I. She was pretty, and was, to some degree, loved by my mother. She made friends more easily and received better treatment at our foster homes. Yet she, like I, was looking for someone who loved her. Her search for love had drawn her into an immoral relationship.

Marie had never shown any interest in God. I would tell her what Christ meant to me, and she would say, "Oh, Dorie, don't talk about that." That saddened me, and I had prayed much for her. Now she was getting married, and I knew that neither she nor her boyfriend had the maturity that a happy, secure marriage needs.

Marie invited me to her wedding, but the people with whom I lived refused to let me go. "She's like your mother," they observed with obvious self-righteousness. "We don't want you to turn out like *her.*"

On the day of the wedding the frustration within me exploded. I knew that my sister needed me perhaps more now than ever, but I was forced to obey the orders of those who could not understand the deep emotional hurts that my sister and I had shared. I threw myself across the bed and again cried to God for strength to bear the heartaches of life. *God, please help Marie and her husband; help them to see that You love them and You care!*

The weeks and months passed, and I began to feel lonely. I decided to take a ferry from San Francisco to visit the orphanage in Oakland. For seven years I had lived in that place, and in a sense it was my home. My friends were there, and I saw them as often as possible.

This time I caught the flu during my brief visit. Dr. Welch came in to see me. "Hi, Dorie," he greeted me, surprised to see me after so long. He had always been nice to me, and now he seemed interested in what I had been doing since leaving the orphanage. We talked for several minutes. I enjoyed the warmth of his friendliness.

Suddenly he asked, "How'd you like to come work for me and take room and board with us?"

"Of course!" I replied. I did not even have to think it over. "I'd love to live with you and Mrs. Welch."

Thankfully, I never had to return to my church foster family. The doctor took care of the legal arrangements, and after my bout with the flu I moved directly into Dr. and Mrs. Welch's beautiful home in Piedmont, near Oakland. My foster family was notified, and they sent all my belongings to my new address.

Lord, am I dreaming? I have a wonderful place to live, and the doctor's going to be my boss! This is too good to be true.

7

Doris, Where Is Your Father?

Walking into the Welches' home was like walking into heaven. The heavy, carved door of their two-story stucco home swung open to reveal a large, tiled entryway. They took me up a winding stairway to my room, a large, bright room, fully carpeted. I would have a double bed and dresser all to myself.

Mrs. Welch gave me the new clothes that had been promised. My heart sank. No pleated skirts with matching sweaters as I had imagined. They were black and white uniforms. I would be a maid!

I didn't dare show my disappointment, for the Welches' home was better than anything I had known. But I was afraid my eyes would be a dead giveaway to my true feelings. *Lord,* I prayed silently. *Let me smile, and don't let them see how I feel.*

My duties were clarified: I would answer the phone, respond to the doorbell, serve meals, and perform many other servant services. I was not accepted as a member of the family, and would not eat meals with them. By now I had come to accept my second-class status, and I supposed I would always have to eat alone.

A few days after I transferred to my new home my personal belongings arrived from the church family where I had stayed for eight months. As I put on one of my dresses, I noticed a note in my pocket. "You're a hypocrite."

53

What did I do to deserve that? I asked the Lord. The next day I found another note. "You ugly thing." I concluded that the family was angry with me because my decision to leave their home had reflected unfavorably on them.

One day I put my hand in the pocket of my sweater and there was another note. "Judas." I burst into tears.

Mrs. Welch heard me. "What's wrong, Doris?"

"Oh, just another one of those notes—"

"What do you mean?" she questioned me.

I tried to avoid explaining, but the doctor's wife persisted. When she heard the full story, she was angry and immediately contacted the juvenile authorities to tell them to investigate my previous foster home. They agreed to do so. I never heard the outcome of that investigation.

Mrs. Welch's concern for me was a pleasant surprise. That was the first time I could remember that anyone took my side when I had a problem. *She really cares,* I thought.

The incident also had a bad effect. Later when I told Mrs. Welch about the power of Christ, she rejected the gospel, citing her deep disappointment in Christians. As an example, she referred to the notes I had found. "Just look at what those Christian people did to you!" she reminded me.

The doctor paid me $2.50 per week, and for the first time in my life I could keep what I earned. White buck shoes were in style and I was determined to buy a pair, the best pair I could find. An exclusive store in downtown Oakland sold them for $10.95, so I saved my money until I could go shopping and pick out the first merchandise I had ever bought: white buck shoes.

The next day I was the proudest sixteen-year-old girl in the school. I'm sure I must have been a sight, my white shoes a glaring contrast to my dingy, outdated dress. But I felt in style.

Although I was a maid in the Welches' home, they provided more love and kindness than I had ever known. They never put me down, but helped me appreciate myself. And they took the time to teach me. They would correct my grammar, giving me confidence in my speech. Mrs. Welch taught me the right way to clean and manage a home. She explained to me the quality of her Duncan Phyfe furniture, her Chippendale breakfront, her Spode china, and her silver. I wanted to learn to appreciate and care for those things, even if I would never own them.

The Welches loved to read, and they shared with me all the books in their library. They also listened to classical music and taught me to appreciate it.

Most of all, they modeled for me a loving home. I would watch them look lovingly at each other and treat each other with kindness. I would watch Mrs. Welch rock her baby daughter and see the tenderness with which she diapered and dressed her. As she cared for that baby, she would teach me all the loving things a mother does.

"Dorie," she would often say. "I can't understand a mother not loving her children." I never pursued the conversation. My eyes would sting as I saw the love I had always wanted. For the first time I began to respect the word *mother*. I had long determined the kind of mother I *wouldn't* be. Now from Mrs. Welch I formed my ideals of the mother I hoped to someday become. Although the Welches lived busy lives, the children always came first. She gave hours to teaching them and caring for them.

Several months after I arrived, I made a sketch of Mrs. Welch's father. She liked it. "Dorie," she said, "you've done many other things around here that have been good, and I've never complimented you for them. I just want you to know I appreciate your work."

I thought I would float out of the room!

I admired Mrs. Welch and observed her closely, trying to

stay clean and neat like she did. She would tell me when I looked nice, so I tried to imitate her.

"Dorie," she called me one day. "I've been thinking about the best advice I could possibly give you." I perked my ears. "It's this: always strive to be a lady."

I'm sure my jaw dropped. I was expecting something big.

"Would you like to know what a real lady is?" she continued.

"Yes ma'am."

"A lady never gets excited, and always keeps her voice low and calm. She is always in control."

Tall and elegant, Mrs. Welch was the picture of a lady. But although I tried hard to follow her wisdom, I often squealed when excited.

During high school I had no boyfriends, nor did I try to attract any. I knew I didn't dress as nicely as the other girls. And I was ashamed that I had no real home, no real family. I thought it would be nice to have a boyfriend someday, but now I felt safer staying at a distance.

While living with the Welches I continued to memorize Scripture and study the Word. Although I was no longer living under duress, I loved the Lord too much to let my relationship with Him slide. He was still my one true Friend. The Welches loaned me a radio, and I listened to any Christian programs I could find.

I began attending a Christian and Missionary Alliance Church about ten miles from the Welches. Incredible though it may seem, I walked until the Welches moved farther away. Then I took the bus part way. Although the church had activities for the young people, I was unable to attend because I lived so far away. I would tell them I worked for a doctor, but I revealed no more of my past. Once I was able to go to a roller skating party. I wasn't very good, and I hit the floor more times than I'd like to count. But I had a great time. I skated only with the girls, however. No boys. That felt safer.

As high school graduation approached, I expected to go alone. I would graduate without fanfare. It would be no big thing.

"Dorie," Dr. Welch surprised me the night before. "When does your commencement exercise begin?"

"Why? Why do you want to know?"

"Why, Dorie, we're coming to see you!" he said.

That night as I walked across the stage, my heart thumped wildly. Hundreds of people clapped routinely. But someone was clapping for *me!*

After graduation I was encouraged to attend the California College of Arts and Crafts. My dream of being a great artist seemed on the verge of reality. That fall with money I had saved, I began an art course, which I thoroughly enjoyed.

Each day I would carry a quarter to school. Ten cents I spent for bus fare. But I had an extra fifteen cents. I could hold change in my hand like everyone else. When the girls would go for a soda, I'd go with them so they could see that I had some change. But I wouldn't buy a soda. I would save my money for an art pencil or supplies.

One of my greatest responsibilities at the Welches' was baby-sitting for their two children, a girl and a boy. The boy was born after I had come to live with them. Those kids loved me, and I loved them. When the doctor and his wife went to conventions they trusted me with their children for days at a time.

I was also given permission to visit Marie. I got her address from the Makins. She and her husband were living in a small basement apartment in San Francisco. More than a year had passed since we stood together in the school yard. She was surprised and happy to see me. The baby was a cute little boy named Norman.

We talked for a couple of hours, catching up on all our news. Marie was very pleased when I held her son and played with him for awhile. Before leaving I shared with her about Jesus Christ and what He meant to me. Again, she brushed me off. "That's not for me. I have my husband and baby. I don't need God."

My heart ached for my sister. As I left I gave her some money to help buy some groceries. They were poor; I wanted so much to help, but I didn't know how.

I tried to tell Mrs. Welch what the Lord meant to me. Although she and the doctor never attended church, she would often enter discussions with me. But her conclusion was always the same. "Dorie, I can see that for you this is good. Your religion has provided stability. But if you had a loving family, you wouldn't need to lean on religion. I have a full and complete life without it. With a husband and children who love me, I have all that I want."

A year passed. Then another. At age nineteen I began to realize that I could not stay with the Welches forever. It had been the kindest of all my experiences, and I knew they appreciated me. Yet I had to ask myself whether I wanted to be a servant for the rest of my life.

Once when the doctor had a party for his colleagues, a guest came into the kitchen where Mrs. Welch and I were working. "I can see that Doris is a good worker. If you ever want to let her go I get first bid!" I knew the lady meant it as a compliment, but it made me wonder whether this would be all I would have to look forward to in life.

One day Mrs. Welch's aunt was visiting. We began talking. "Doris, you've got to get away from this," she said.

"But they need me. I don't want to upset them by leaving," I protested.

"Oh, they would get over it, dear," the kindly older woman assured me.

The aunt decided to talk to Mrs. Welch about the matter.

I was frightened. *What if the Welches ask me to leave; where would I go?* Mrs. Welch came to me in tears, assuring me that they wanted me to stay but also giving me freedom to leave if I wanted to.

For weeks I prayed about what I should do. Then one day the doctor startled me with a question no one had ever asked. "Doris, where is your father?"

Scattered thoughts passed through my mind. Obviously, I had a father somewhere, but where he was or who he was had never concerned me. Years earlier I had heard rumors that he lived in Tulsa, Oklahoma, but I knew nothing beyond that.

"Why don't we try to find out some information about him?" Dr. Welch suggested. He walked briskly up the stairs, and I followed cautiously behind him into his office. He sat down on the huge, brown leather easy chair and began dialing the long-distance operator in Tulsa. In a moment he said, "Hello. I'm a medical doctor and am interested in locating a Mr. Duckworth. Do you have a Duckworth listed in the directory? A Mr. L. Duckworth?" A brief pause followed. I held my breath.

"Yes, we do—would you like his number?" came the operator's voice.

"No. I just wanted to know if he lives there." With that he hung up the receiver.

"Well, I think you should find your father's address and write him a letter," the doctor suggested.

That evening I composed a letter to a man I did not know, asking if, perchance, he might be my father. I included a bit of history: how I had grown up in an orphanage, and who my mother was. Then I added a brief sketch of what had happened since then. In conclusion I said that I had recently thought about him and wondered what he looked like. I was curious to know whether he was my father.

The telephone company let me use an out-of-state directory. I copied Mr. L. Duckworth's address carefully onto the envelope. *This is so strange,* I thought. *What if this man is not my father? I must know, though. It's worth the risk.*

As I dropped the letter into the mailbox, I breathed a prayer that God would take it to the right man, my father.

8

Sir, Are You My Father?

After mailing the letter I gave little thought to what I had done. Probably if Mr. L. Duckworth was my father, he wouldn't answer me. He had had years to contact me, why should he do so now?

Two weeks passed. The doctor and his wife were seated at opposite ends of their long mahogany table, when the doorbell rang. I left the dining room, walked through the hallway, and opened the heavy oak door. The mailman had brought a letter, airmail, special delivery. I signed my name for it, as I had often done previously for the Welches' letters. As I turned to walk back toward the dining room, I glanced at the envelope, and my eyes caught my name! I screamed so loudly that the doctor and his wife jumped up from the table and collided as they rushed through the narrow dining room door.

"Doris, what in the world is wrong?"

"I got a letter!" I shouted, forgetting to be a lady.

"Then open it!"

Suddenly, I was all thumbs.

"Let me open it," Dr. Welch offered, having regained his composure. Only then did I look at the return address and realized it was from Mr. Duckworth. I was shaking. Perhaps I had said some things that may have hurt him. And possibly, this man was not even my father at all!

Rather than read it, I asked the doctor to just show me

how it was signed. He turned it over to reveal three letters almost a half inch high—DAD.

"Dad! Dad!" I breathed the word aloud and then to myself. All my emotions came unglued. I raced up the stairs, hurried into my bedroom, closed the door, and began to read. Tears streamed down my cheeks as I read and re-read those four pages. I studied them, analyzed them, and memorized them.

He said that when he read my letter he had had difficulty controlling his emotions. Memories of the past began to flood his mind, and he was glad to hear I was well. The letter ended by encouraging me to write to him again.

The next day I dropped a letter in the mailbox—air-mail, special delivery. I had decided not to include a picture of myself, certain that if he saw me, he would not want me. Nor did I ask him for a picture; I thought if he looked like me, I might blame him for my ugly appearance. It seemed best that we keep writing without such specific identification.

One day just after supper the phone rang. In the absence of the doctor, I answered it. "Could I speak to Doris, please?" asked a male voice. My mind went blank. I had no idea who it could be.

"This is her," I replied, not bothering to correct my grammar.

"Doris, honey."

I momentarily dropped the receiver. No one had ever spoken such words to me before. "Doris, are you there, honey? This is your dad." It was the most beautiful voice I had ever heard.

But I was scared. I was talking with a stranger, and he was asking me to come halfway across the United States to visit him.

"No, Dad," I protested. "If you'd see me, you wouldn't want me anyway."

"Don't be silly. Of course I'd want you."

Then perhaps he was having second thoughts. He offered to pay only half my fare, and I could earn the rest.

That night I prayed with mixed emotions. I was delirious with joy—a man, my father, wanted to see me. But I was afraid that this new relationship might pry me away from God. Would the joy of meeting my earthly father overshadow fellowship with my heavenly Father?

Several days passed before I realized that my real fear was that my father would reject me if he saw me. *Maybe it's better that I not meet him than visit him and have him disown me.* But I couldn't resist his invitation. Maybe he would love me. That possibility was worth a trip to Oklahoma.

Since the semester at art school was not over, I decided to wait six weeks before leaving for Tulsa. Before I left, I saw Marie for the last time. I had been visiting her periodically over the past year. When I mentioned that I had made connections with our father and hoped to visit him, she turned to me in bitterness and said, "That's OK for you, but I don't care about him. He never cared about me." I couldn't persuade her otherwise; her heart was filled with hatred.

At last the day had arrived. Bus ticket in hand, I boarded for Tulsa. The doctor and his wife had given me an old suitcase and had tied it with a belt. With their best wishes, I left Californa for the long trip east.

On the bus I began to wonder how I would recognize my father at the depot. In my communication with him I was careful not to suggest that I wear a carnation or any certain color of dress or jacket, for I fully expected rejection. If he identified me at a distance and didn't like what he saw, he might walk away and I'd be left alone. Therefore, I had avoided discussing how we would identify each other. I would just have to wait and see.

The miles seemed endless. I had never been so far away from home before, alone in a world of strangers. I was tense as my destination got closer. My emotions took roller-coaster highs. I was both scared and excited!

By the time I stepped into the crowded station, I had decided to pick out the most handsome man in the room and assume that he was my father. As I elbowed my way through the crowd, my eyes scanned the large room. There, leaning against a huge pillar was a tall, impressive-looking man with dark hair. The closer I got, the better he looked. I promptly put my suitcase down beside him. Then with an abundant supply of gall and tactlessness, I stood at point-blank range and asked, "Sir, are you my father?"

"Well, I guess I am," he replied sheepishly. Like a flash, I was in his strong arms. My father's eyes were moist, and I was weeping. I had never been hugged before.

We drove to Archer Street in an upper middle-class neighborhood. He pulled into the driveway of a two-story white brick home framed with flowers and a perfectly manicured lawn. My dad was a realtor, and I could see he had done well. I felt proud of him.

He introduced me to his wife, Blanche. After we became acquainted they invited me to stay with them permanently. I accepted. Unexpectedly, I felt at ease and comfortable. I was really happy. My father seemed to love me!

He was a kind man who tried desperately to make up for some of the ugliness of the past. He expressed surprise that I, the one least loved of the two girls, should initiate a contact and that we should still share a part of our lives together. He introduced me as his daughter to his friends. Never did he attempt to hide my identity. Sometimes he was a bit uneasy, perhaps chagrined that his past had caught up with him. But there was no doubt that he wanted the best for me, and he encouraged me to get a job as an artist.

The Douglas Aircraft Company needed an illustrator,

With my father in Tulsa. (1943)

and I fit the bill. The architect would give me plans and I would sketch a diagram of how the completed equipment was expected to look. My job was lucrative. I charged by the square inch (my drawing board was four feet by six feet). I was convinced that this was a stepping-stone to my eventual career in art.

I was friendly with the other girls in the office, and I often went out to lunch with them. But none became a close friend. I was so taken with getting to know my father that other friendships seemed unimportant. Being accepted by him was the height of my world.

I stayed in Tulsa for two years. Only once during that time did I ask my father about the past. Why had we been placed in an orphanage? Why hadn't he visited us, or tried to find us? My father spoke with difficulty about those days, and I sensed that such a discussion would harm our present relationship. We agreed that the past would be best forgotten.

If a discussion of the past was out of place, there was one matter that was completely taboo, that of God. "Father," I began one day after careful thought, "before I came to visit you I did have one Friend."

"Who?" he asked, obviously interested. Slowly I explained how I had accepted Christ in the orphanage years before, and that although no one else loved me, I knew that God did.

My father resented such talk and let me know that he had no time for God or religion. Whatever I had discovered was fine for me but not for him. He flatly rejected any further communication about God. I attended church and kept my fellowship with God alive. But I could share none of this with my father.

Dad's lack of interest in God erected a barrier between us. He was kind to me, encouraged me in my vocation, and obviously tried to atone for some of the wrongs of the past.

But he also began pulling me in his direction, urging me to adopt the standards and social practices of the world. He couldn't understand why I didn't want to attend movies, dance, or take a drink. Increasingly, I knew that I would have to decide: I would either say yes to God and leave my father, or say no to God and stay. The choice was that clear.

One question kept popping into my mind: *Who loved you when no one else did?* My father had not visited me in the orphanage. He made no effort to find me, although he could have done so easily. I had initiated our contact. Through years of beatings, hunger, and rejection, I had only one dependable Friend: God. He was my Father when I had none; He made my mother's insults bearable, and preserved my sanity during years of cruelty. God had done all this for me, and more. My decision boiled down to this: I had to choose between my earthly father, who had neglected me, and my heavenly Father, who had lovingly adopted me.

Although the issues were clear, the choice was not easy. The past two years had been enjoyable. For the first time in my life I had had a feeling of security, a sense of belonging. My job was delightful, and my freedom boosted my badly eroded sense of self-worth.

I opted for my heavenly Father. Without giving details, I told my father that I would have to go back to California to make a decision. I promised I would return someday to tell him what I had decided. He neither pressed for more information nor tried to dissuade me. Whatever I wanted was fine. He would not stand in my way.

With a heavy heart I returned to California.

9

Lord, You Wouldn't!

I arrived in California just after my twenty-first birthday. I was pursuing my career in art. Yet for all my apparent success, I was restless. God, I suspected, had a plan for my life. But it was a mystery to me.

Dr. and Mrs. Welch welcomed me when I returned to San Francisco. They were pleased (more accurately, surprised) that I had had a lucrative job in Tulsa. They suggested that I apply for a job at Moore Business Forms in Emeryville, just outside Oakland. I was accepted for drawing the plans that architects created.

I moved my belongings into the Blue Triangle Motel, not far from my new job. I cooked my own meals, kept up my small apartment, and paid my own rent. For the first time I, Doris Duckworth, was getting along alone in the world.

Even so, I was dissatisfied. God was speaking to me about committing myself to Him completely for whatever He had planned. I was scared. Maybe God didn't want me to be an artist after all. Art was my talent, my only profession. *Lord, I can't do anything else,* I told Him, hoping He'd be convinced.

There was one occupation, however, from which I hoped God would spare me—missionary service. My dislike for this career dated back to my days at the orphanage when I attended the Gospel Tabernacle. There at a conference I hastily concluded that missionaries were colorless nonentities, people who were shipped overseas because they could not make a decent showing in America. When they stood to speak they looked like dried prunes. *They look as bad as I do,* I concluded. To top it off, missionaries couldn't have the comforts that I had been denied all my life. It didn't seem fair. My last desire was to be a missionary. And my second last desire was to marry a preacher. Becoming a missionary meant joining a group of second-rate saints; marrying a preacher meant being on display for the rest of my life.

Evangelist Hyman Appelman was having meetings at the Civic Auditorium in Oakland. The night I attended he closed his message saying, "What is it—one more dance, one more fling, and then you are going to come back to God?"

For a moment I thought he had read my mind. My purpose in coming back to California was to give my life fully to God, but I wanted one last fling, or at least the assurance that God would let me keep my career in art. And now God was closing in on me. Was I willing to give my life completely and irrevocably to Him?

When the invitation was given, I walked to the front to say no to my plans and yes to God. But my commitment, though sincere, was not complete. I was saying that God could do with me what He wished—except lead me into missionary service or make me marry a preacher.

A few weeks later a missionary convention was slated at the Gospel Tabernacle. Early Sunday morning a delegation of church members drove to the San Francisco harbor to welcome several missionaries who had just arrived on the boat named *Gripsholm.* The group arrived at the church just in time for the morning service, still wearing Red Cross jackets and tennis shoes. They looked as bad as I remembered looking in the orphanage. My suspicions were confirmed.

Among those asked to speak that morning was Darlene

Deibler, who had just returned from a Japanese internment camp in New Guinea. After Pearl Harbor, Japanese troups had swarmed into the Dutch East Indies, and six Alliance missionaries were murdered. The missionary statesman Dr. Robert Jaffray, along with his wife and a young couple, Charles and Darlene Deibler, moved to a health resort, hoping to avoid political harassment.

On March 13, 1942, Japanese troops arrested the missionaries and confined them to police barracks. Then inexplicably, Dr. Jaffray was permitted to remain with the women while Darlene's husband, Charles, was sent to a concentration camp, where he experienced brutality, rotten food, and disease. He died on August 28, 1942.

Darlene, confined in the barracks a hundred miles away, did not learn of her husband's death until two months later. A fellow prisoner smuggled the news to her and gave her a pencil sketch of her husband's grave.

She had lost everything. All her belongings were destroyed. Even their marriage certificate had been so badly charred in the bombings that it disintegrated when Darlene picked it up.

Now she stood before the packed church. "Young people," she said, "it cost me everything to serve the Lord." She paused, then added, "For Jesus' sake, I'd do it again." Solemnly, she sat down.

Grown men sitting in the pews ahead of me wept openly. I felt a hand on my shoulder. Two women were sitting on either side of me, and for a fleeting moment I thought one of them had leaned forward. But I knew they had not stirred. Only then did I realize that God had touched me.

God, You wouldn't! You wouldn't goof up my life! You wouldn't ask me to be one of them! I have plans. I have dreams!

But God can be neither refused nor ignored. He was speaking to me, and I knew He wanted me to be a missionary to the country Darlene Deibler had just spoken about: New Guinea.

After the meeting I walked downstairs to the prayer room to settle the matter. *Yes, for Your sake, Jesus, I'll do it.* The decision was overwhelming. "Lord," I prayed intensely, "let me know beyond all doubt that You're talking to me. I want to know I'm really hearing Your voice. I don't want this decision just to be emotional."

That evening Dr. Paul Rood brought the final message of the convention. He concluded by telling a story of a girl who refused to become a missionary because she wouldn't give up the close ties with her earthly father.

Had someone told him about me? That description fit me exactly! My father, for all his faults, belonged to me, and I to him. He was the only one in the world who loved me. Try as I might, I could not tear myself from that relationship. Dr. Rood's concluding illustration was the clincher. God was telling me that I had heard Him correctly in the morning service: He wanted me in New Guinea.

When I went to the altar that evening, Darlene Deibler knelt and put her arm around me. Together we prayed, and I promised, "Lord, I'll go."

A few days after the convention, Darlene asked a favor of me. She had heard that I was an artist and wondered if I would make a copy of a special drawing.

She handed me a piece of paper the size of a post card. It had been folded and refolded so many times that it almost fell apart when I opened it. Laying it gently on the table in my room I noticed that it was a pencil sketch of a mound of dirt, topped by a cross with the name "Charles Russel Deibler." In Dutch the bottom caption read, "God takes the best."

The picture had been drawn by a young man who had been converted under Charles's ministry when they were together in the internment camp. He had sketched a picture of Charles's grave and given it to Darlene. The grave site was in a pig sty.

As I gathered my art equipment, I breathed a prayer that God would help me sketch every line accurately. And in a voice almost audible, God asked me whether I would help take the gospel to New Guinea.

Lord, I can't fill his shoes. He was a martyr.

"I'm not asking you to fill his shoes, but to walk in the same way."

From then on my energy was concentrated on preparing myself for missionary service. The Christian and Missionary Alliance Church had their Bible college in St. Paul, Minnesota, so I planned to attend.

While preparing, I grew close to Darlene. Although she was often out of town speaking, she pursued my friendship. She was about twelve years my senior, yet I knew she cared about me as a person, not just as a potential missionary.

One day Darlene and her mother made a surprise visit to my tiny apartment. "Dorie, you're moving in with us," they announced. Without further discussion, they gathered all my belongings. When we arrived at their home, Darlene's mother said, "Daddy, tell Dorie what you planned."

"From now on," he said, "we're not Mr. and Mrs. McIntoch. We're Mother and Daddy Mac."

I gasped. Someone had chosen me! At last, at age twenty-one, I belonged. Darlene and I shared a bedroom and became close friends. Gradually I trusted her with my whole story.

While living with Mother and Daddy Mac, I unexpectedly learned of my mother's whereabouts: she was working as a waitress in the cafeteria section of a large drugstore. Almost five years had passed since I had seen her, and I preferred not to meet her again. Darlene, however, encouraged me to see my mother one more time. My reluctance was overcome by her persistence. "Would you go if I came with you?" she asked.

I agreed, on the condition that we would see her only at a distance and not necessarily greet her. We walked in between the long counters of the drugstore until we came to the cafeteria, where several patrons sat, waiting to be served. Silently we stood behind the perfume counter, watching. Then my mother appeared. Darlene whispered, "Do you want to speak to her?" My answer was no.

For a fleeting moment I wondered what would happen if I stepped to the counter and said, "Hello, Mother!" But I resisted the temptation. Any desire to run to her, hug her, or claim her had left me. I felt no bitterness; I just knew she would use the occasion to disown me one last time, and I didn't want that.

Perhaps three or four minutes passed as I watched her; it was like taking one long look into the past. One memory after another rolled irresistibly into my mind like so many waves on the seashore. There she was before me—my mother. My heart yearned that the past could have been different. She was smiling, obviously enjoying her job. *She doesn't care that she's got a daughter out in the world somewhere.*

Reality crashed upon me like a huge breaker. As much as I would have liked to, I couldn't change any of the past. The Lord had a future for me, I knew, but I could go forward only if I could let go of the past. I would have to accept that the cruel things had happened, and put them under Christ's blood. Standing there, I chose to sever the relationships of the past. I was ready to go on.

Darlene took my arm, and we turned and walked away. That was the last time I saw my mother. I sat in the car ten or fifteen minutes without speaking. My feelings went too deep for tears or words. Though I still felt the sting of rejection, I felt no bitterness. God spared me from that. I felt a deep peace that God loved me and would guide my future.

Before I left for Minnesota, one other responsibility weighed heavily on my mind. I owed my father an explanation about my decision to become a missionary. I arranged to give him the news in person.

When it came time to leave, Mother and Daddy Mac and Darlene came to see me off. As I left they said, "If you ever get lonesome and feel like you need Mother or Daddy to talk to, we're here."

10

You Are Not My Daughter

As I neared Tulsa, my excitement grew. It had been ten months since I left. I imagined how proud Dad would be when he heard I was going to do something profitable with my life. Even though he didn't share my love for God, I thought he would share my joy and happiness.

When I arrived at the train station, I took a cab to my father's house. As we turned the last corner, I could hardly wait. Hastily paying the driver, I jumped out with my suitcase and ran up the sidewalk. Dad was sitting on the front porch. As he recognized me, he stood slowly and walked to the edge of the stairs.

Slinging aside my suitcase, I grabbed him in a big hug. "Dad!"

"Hi, honey." He stretched out his arms and we embraced.

My father looked thin and sallow. I knew he had a severe heart condition, and it was obvious he was in great discomfort. Slowly he lowered himself into the rocker. I sat on the edge of the porch close to him. He asked me about my trip and how I was doing. Then his mood changed and he became contemplative.

"Dorie," he said slowly. "All my life I've had a philosophy to live by. But you know—" He paused as if groping for the right words. "You know, now I don't have a philosophy to die by. And I'm dying."

I held my breath. I had been earnestly praying for him, asking God to soften his heart toward Christ. Maybe my

77

prayers would be answered. My heart aching with both deep love and sadness, I shared with him the best news I knew.

"Dad, Christ is the only one who can prepare us for death—you can accept Him."

"*No!* I didn't want Him when I was healthy, and I don't want Him now."

"Dad," I pleaded. "Dad, you *can* accept Him now."

"No, Doris. No!"

I paused, not believing. My mind was reeling but I had to go on. "Dad, I've come to tell you something—God has called me to be a missionary to New Guinea to tell others about Christ. I hope to go to Bible school this fall."

Ill as he was, he stood; his eyes stared aimlessly past me. Then he turned to face the back of the porch. "If that's what you plan to do, then don't unpack your suitcase. Call a cab right now and go back to California. From this moment on you are not my daughter!"

"Dad, you don't mean it!"

"Yes, I do. I never want to see you again!"

My knees weakened, and my heart beat wildly. My stomach rose to my throat. Tears tried to tumble from my eyes, but I forced them back. I was sure I couldn't be hearing right. The finality in my father's voice scared me. There was nothing left to say. I walked slowly to the front door, hesitating, hoping my dad would turn to me and tell me he had made a terrible mistake. He didn't move. I went in and dialed a cab. When I returned to the porch, he was still standing with his back toward me. Several minutes passed as we stood silently. I tried to hug him, but he stiffened.

"Dad, I still love you."

He did not reply. Nor would he turn around. A moment later the cab pulled in front of the house. I grabbed my suitcase and got into the back seat. As the car pulled away, my father was still standing with his back toward the street.

That was the last time I saw my father alive.

Rain splashed against the windows of the train as it pulled out of Tulsa for the long trip back to California. The overcast sky and approaching darkness added to the gloom that weighed heavily on my heart. Every chug of the old steam engine seemed to say, *You're all alone—You're all alone—You're all alone—*I wept openly, fumbling with my moist handkerchief in my hands. For a moment I thought indeed I was alone. I had consulted God about this trip. I had prayed regularly for my father, and now it was all over.

Lord, he was the only person in the world who ever loved me. How could he do this to me? My father had rejected me deliberately, irrevocably. Worse, he had rejected Christ for the last time.

Perhaps an hour went by before I had the presence of mind to remember that God had not left me. Years earlier I had memorized a verse that now came to mind, "I will never leave thee, nor forsake thee. So that we may boldly say, The Lord is my helper, and I will not fear what man shall do unto me" (Hebrews 13:5*b*-6). Bits and pieces of Romans 8:38-39 came to me, "For I am persuaded, that neither death, nor life, nor angels, nor principalities, nor powers, nor things present, nor things to come, nor height, nor depth, nor any other creature, shall be able to separate us from the love of God, which is in Christ Jesus our Lord." And at that moment the warmth of the love of God comforted me. No, I was not alone, not at all.

My mother regretted that she ever bore me. My father was unconcerned about me through my formative years, and now he had disowned me. Only one Friend had not abandoned me—Jesus Christ.

Someone has said that when you have nothing left but

God, you realize that God is enough. God had stood beside me when no one else wanted me; He was not going to abandon me now. God would have to heal the emotional pain that throbbed through my body.

11

Here Come the GI's!

At the St. Paul Bible Institute in September 1946 the girls in the dormitory had cause for excitement. Handsome and eligible GI's were returning from the war. And some of them were enrolled for the fall semester. One in particular caused a stir: he was tall, dark, and handsome, and he spoke with a Texas drawl.

"You just wait. Some girl will ruin him," I predicted in the middle of a dormitory discussion, attended by an all-female cast of GI admirers. Modesty and lack of a sense of self-worth prevented me from thinking that I would fulfill my own prophecy! But a small miracle happened.

Lloyd Van Stone was born and reared in Houston, Texas. His father owned a small grocery store and lost virtually everything in the Depression. Later he worked long hours in a bakery, often from 2:00 A.M. to 5:00 P.M. Lloyd's parents were honest, moral, and hard working, but they were not Christians.

When Lloyd was fifteen, his uncle Herbert invited him to a Bible club for boys. Uncle Herbert held the club each week at his home. Not long after that a missionary convention came to the Christian and Missionary Alliance Church in Houston. Lloyd's cousin John attended and became a believer. He told Lloyd that he had been saved. Lloyd couldn't understand what *saved* could possibly mean. He thought John must have fallen into the river and someone rescued him.

81

When P. R. Hyde, a Bible teacher, came to the church, Lloyd attended the meetings with apprehension. On the third night Hyde gave an invitation to accept Christ. A woman behind Lloyd tapped his shoulder and asked, "Son, are you saved?"

"Yes," Lloyd replied, somewhat embarrassed. He was lying. When the pastor took his hand and asked him the same question, he was cornered. Weary of running from God, he accepted Christ as Savior that night.

A couple of years passed. Lloyd had gone with a group of young people to be at a missions conference in Nyack, New York. Dr. Turnball presented the challenge of missionary work in Borneo. That afternoon Lloyd promised God that he would go anywhere in the world to share the gospel.

In 1943, Lloyd was assigned to the First Cavalry Division in the Pacific. The recruits were not told where they were headed. Lloyd believed they were on their way to India or Burma, but much to their surprise, the ship arrived on the north coast of New Guinea. He was stationed at the Admiralty Islands.

When Lloyd saw the nationals with their long, unkempt hair, he understood why the GI's dubbed them "fuzzy wuzzies." He was so repulsed that he could not understand how missionaries could live among those primitive peoples. They were dirty, undisciplined, and barbaric. When the war was over and the fighting stopped in New Guinea, Lloyd was glad to leave the country that he hoped he would never see again.

God had other plans. At a camp meeting in Arlington, Texas, in June of 1946, Lloyd was meditating alone in the empty tent. "And there," he says, "God asked if I would return to New Guinea as a missionary. I yielded."

So it was that both Lloyd and I enrolled in the freshman class of 1946 at the St. Paul Bible Institute. Although we knew each other casually during the first semester, our courtship began in January. Both of us were chosen to give speeches at the city-wide World Missionary Conference, and our instructor asked us to practice our speeches together. We thought it was an excellent idea.

One night Lloyd had a dream in which he saw himself marry me! Promptly, but also fearfully, he made up his mind to ask me out for a date.

"Dorie," he began, "let's go to the hamburger shop after dinner tonight."

"That sounds great," I answered, trying desperately to conceal my happiness. *This is my first date,* I reminded myself.

"I'll meet you in the lobby at seven o'clock," Lloyd added.

At first I told no one that he'd asked me out. I was afraid someone would sneer and say, "How come *you?*" I carefully combed my closet for the big event. I looked my best in my navy skirt and light blue blouse, I decided. At five minutes to seven I was still in my room frantically getting ready.

"Dorie! Your date's here!" one of the girls called from downstairs.

O Lord, it's so nice to have someone waiting for me.

As we walked out into Minnesota's blustery winter, I was afraid I'd slip on the ice and look foolish. I welcomed the opportunity to slip my arm through Lloyd's. At the hamburger shop we sat across from each other, exchanged meaningful glances, and talked. *I hope our hands touch when we pass the ketchup.* We talked about school and our plans for the summer. He told me about his home life, and I told him I'd grown up in Oakland, had worked for a doctor, and had attended art school. How grateful I was that he didn't press for details.

After our long conversation, we began walking back to

school. The night was clear, the stars brilliant. He took my hand, then began looking for the Big Dipper. *Is this what I've been missing? It's great!*

We arrived back at the dorm past closing hour, and the night watchman had to let us in. "I can tell where you've been," he teased. "I smell the onions of the hamburger shop."

We burst out laughing. Right there Lloyd turned to me and asked, "Hey, can I have another date?"

"Sure."

"OK, Stinkie."

So I answered, "Good night, Stinker." And that's what we've called each other ever since. I always sign my cards to him, "Stinkie OHILY." That's our code for "Oh how I love you."

Once when Lloyd came to the dorm for a date, no one was on the switchboard. So he got on the board and sang out, "Calling Stinkie! Are you ready!" All the doors opened. I could have died. But there he stood, grinning and waiting for me.

By the time school let out, our friendship had grown. Before leaving for the summer we agreed to write. I went on tour with Dr. Strohm, president of the college, and a girls' quartet. The quartet would sing, and I would speak, representing the students who were preparing for missionary service. Lloyd was doing Christian service in the Ozarks.

We wrote regularly, sharing our thoughts and telling each other about our meetings. To disguise his letters, Lloyd always drew a Big Dipper in the corner rather than put his return address. In his last letter that summer he said, "I've been thinking about us. Let me know when you're coming in, and I'll be at the station to meet you."

Sure enough, Lloyd was waiting for me at the St. Paul

railway station. *I can hardly wait for him to kiss me,* I thought as the train came to a screeching halt. Moments later I was in his strong arms, and he kissed me. "It feels just as good as I thought it would," I whispered to him.

Enroute to the school we walked past a jewelry store.

"Let's stop to look at rings. I want to get one for you," Lloyd blurted without warning. Disbelievingly, I glanced up into his face, and he whispered those three short words I had longed for so deeply, "I love you." Then he kissed me again.

When I got to the school I rushed into the girls' dormitory. I couldn't go to my room and meet the friends I had not seen all summer—I was crying and they would demand an explanation. So I climbed up a stairway into a large storage room in the attic. I hid behind the trunks and suitcases and turned on my flashlight. I began to pray aloud, opening my Bible at random at the same time. "Lord, how could You be so good to let a man love me? He doesn't care that I'm ugly. He just loves me! Lord, this is too good to be true."

The flashlight fell on my open Bible. I looked down and was amazed to read these verses in Matthew 19:29-30, "And every one that hath forsaken houses, or brethren, or sisters, or father, or mother, or wife, or children, or lands, for my name's sake, shall receive an hundredfold, and shall inherit everlasting life. But many that are first shall be last; and the last shall be first."

We spent as much time together as we could during the next school year. As we got to know one another better we were more certain that God had led us together.

That Christmas we visited his parents in Houston. They accepted me immediately. In fact, their attitude seemed to say, "Treat her right, Lloyd, or you'll answer to us." I couldn't help noticing how kindly he treated his mother.

Surely the Lord had chosen His best for me. Christmas morning I opened the most beautiful gift—an engagement ring from the man I loved. We set the date for June 15.

I couldn't afford a wedding dress, but I didn't want to ask. When I returned to school, however, a married friend said, "Dorie, I've been thinking about something, and I feel it's from the Lord. I have my wedding dress here and think it will fit you. You may wear it if you like." It fit perfectly. A cousin gave me a veil. Several families in the Alliance church in Oakland gave me a shower and also gave money for wedding expenses.

We were married in the Alliance church in Houston. When the day arrived, I awoke and prayed, *Lord, make us a blessing, and make our home an example of what Your love really means. If You give us children, make them a blessing and honor to Your name.* Then I pinched myself. *Lord, is this really real?*

I felt like a queen on my wedding day. *Lord, if You can make me beautiful for one day, make it today.* And I felt beautiful! I didn't know how to find Marie, nor did I want to. This day was too perfect to spoil it with hurts from the past.

I had often wondered who would escort me down the aisle. Lloyd's uncle Herbert, a bachelor, volunteered. "Oh, Uncle Herbert," I said as I hugged him. "I'd just love to have you." As we started down the aisle, Lloyd winked at me. I quickened my pace, dragging Uncle Herbert with me. Fortunately the organist stepped up the tempo so we wouldn't beat her.

We rented a small apartment near the institute and completed our final year of school together. In May, 1949, we graduated. From there we went to Houston to await the birth of our son, Burney. Soon after his birth on July 6, 1949, we accepted an invitation to pastor a small Alliance

With Lloyd—my husband, best friend, source of inspira-
tion, and tower of strength. (1975)

church in Lubbock, Texas. Our first offering was five cents!

If someone had told me during those fearful days in the orphanage that I would someday be genuinely happy, I would not have believed him. But here I was, married to a wonderful, competent husband. I was the mother of a precious baby. God had done abundantly above all that I could ask or think and blessed my life beyond measure.

Yet our goal remained clearly before us: New Guinea.

12

Dad, I Loved You

During the years I was a student at St. Paul Bible Institute I often thought of my father. Despite the fact that he had disowned me, I hoped he'd had a change of heart by now and would accept me once more. I prayed and asked God what I should do. One day I called him long distance from Minneapolis.

"Dad, this is Doris."

I heard a click at the other end of the line. Later I wrote him a letter but received no reply.

After my engagement to Lloyd I telephoned my father again. "Dad, please don't hang up until I've told you something important. Dad, I'm engaged to a wonderful man who loves me dearly. I wish you could meet him. We are going to serve the Lord together as missionaries. But don't worry, Dad, he'll take good care of me."

At the other end, my father uttered but one word, "Good-bye."

That was hard to take, but with Lloyd at my side to love and reassure me I was able to leave it in the past. After our son Burney was born, I longed for my father to see his grandchild, but I decided against making contact with him. The birth of my child was the beginning of a new life for me, too. The past would have to be forgotten and forgiven. I knew my father had a will of steel. Nothing, not even a grandson, could pry him loose from his hatred for God and his insistence that I not become a missionary.

At that time we didn't know whether my dad was dead or alive. Four years had passed since he and I had met on the front porch of his home. We suspected that when he died, we would not know about it.

But God planned otherwise. As missionaries under appointment by the Christian and Missionary Alliance, we were encouraged to attend their annual meeting in Toronto in May, 1950. Although I was expecting our second child, we decided to go.

We had no car for the long trip, but a pastor from Tulsa had invited us to drive up to Toronto with him. En route back to Texas, we stopped at St. Louis, Missouri, and from there the pastor phoned his wife in Tulsa. She told him that she had just read of the death of my father in the local newspaper. The wake was scheduled for the next day, the funeral for the day after. In great haste we continued our journey to Tulsa, hoping to arrive in time for the wake and funeral.

The next day we drove to the funeral home. My heart began to pound; I was submerged by waves of emotion. I tried to think of the good times I had had with my father, but mostly I remembered that day on the front porch when he disowned me.

A moment later we walked into the lobby of the funeral home. "Sir, could you tell us where Lewis Duckworth's body is?"

He pointed to a sign near the door of one of the rooms. Yes, there it was, "Lewis Duckworth." I opened the guest book and signed my name under the heading *Daughters*. The funeral director was chagrined.

"He didn't have any children."

"Oh, yes. I'm his daughter."

"Well, you can't come in, or it will upset the family. If you want to see him, you'll have to come back just before we close tonight."

My father was true to his word. Because of his prominence in the community, his death notice was on the front page of the local paper. Among other things it said, "He had no children." The funeral director wanted to respect my father's wishes.

As we turned to leave, I saw one of my aunts coming from my father's room. She and I had become acquainted during the time I lived with my dad in Tulsa. We spoke briefly, and she agreed that it would be best if I were to leave. However, she asked for the phone number at the home where we were staying.

Sadly, Lloyd and I drove back to the home of the minister who had taken us to Toronto and back. An hour later the telephone rang; it was the aunt I had met in the funeral home.

"Doris, I think it is best if you don't attend the funeral. You know, there were strong feelings against you—"

"Yes, I know," I said.

"But I've always liked you," she assured me. "In fact, I have some things I think your father would want you to have. I'll bring them over."

In a short while my aunt arrived. She gave me a box of books that had meant a lot to my father. Among them was a series called *Great Philosophers*.

That evening Lloyd and I drove to the funeral home to see my father. "Lloyd, I'm sorry that this is the way you have to meet—"

"That's OK, honey, I understand." My husband had always been very kind about the matter of my family; now he was a great comfort to me.

We quietly slipped into the room, and there lay my father. He was dressed in a dubonnet robe, his hands folded across his chest. Even in death he was handsome, with rugged features and dark complexion.

As I stared at his lifeless body, the emotions I had bottled up for so many years poured out. *Dad, I loved you! I loved you! I loved you!* I sobbed. We stood there for several minutes.

Lloyd gently slipped his arm around me. "Dorie, I'm glad he didn't want you; if he had, I would never have found you." I thought I might collapse, but Lloyd helped me walk out of the funeral home and put me in the car.

As we drove away, the last words my dad had spoken to me throbbed in my ears, "I never want to see you again. You are not my daughter."

The next day Lloyd went to the funeral, but I kept my promise and did not attend. That afternoon I recalled all the times Lloyd and I had prayed earnestly for my father. I had felt confident that someday he would still accept me and, most of all, accept Christ as his Savior. *Lord, how could You let him die without accepting your forgiveness?*

The Bible tells us that God works all events for ultimate good, and that even evil is a part of His total plan. That is true, but it did not seem to make it easier for me to stand beside the casket of someone I loved, someone who had blatantly rejected Jesus Christ. To my knowledge my father refused God's forgiveness to the very end. If so, he and I shall never meet again for all eternity. The conversation on the front porch of his home will have been our last; there will not be another good-bye, for there will not be another hello—forever.

Several months later, on October 5, 1950, God gave Burney a baby sister. We named her Darlene, in a loving tribute to Darlene Deibler, who had become one of my dearest friends.

A year passed at the little church in Lubbock. We had become restless and decided that the time had come to take a giant step with God. We had not yet been appointed to New Guinea, but we believed that if we raised our own support, the Christian and Missionary Alliance would *have* to send us.

We resigned our church and drove to California, speaking along the way in any church that would have us. From there we went to Minnesota and in just a few weeks had raised enough money for one year of missionary work. We sent the funds directly to the Alliance headquarters in New York and promptly were notified that we had been appointed to New Guinea.

The anticipation of the future helped dull the emotional pain of the past. My father's death ended all earthly ties with my relatives. Now I had Lloyd, two beautiful children, and above all, God. *Lord, with Your help, we'll keep moving ahead.*

13

New Guinea, Here We Come!

During Lloyd's orientation classes in preparation for military service, he saw a map that showed different insects representing diseases in each country of the world. He casually observed that New Guinea seemed to have them all! Yet God was calling, and we were listening.

Following a brief stint in Wycliffe's Summer Institute of Linguistics in Norman, Oklahoma, we left New York harbor for the long trip east. Leaders from the Christian and Missionary Alliance Church were on hand to bid us Godspeed as we boarded the freighter *Soes Dyjk,* which slowly pushed its way into the Atlantic. We spent our days aboard relaxing and enjoying the fellowship of two other missionary couples.

Three months later, in March, 1952, we arrived in Indonesia and transferred to a smaller ship that brought us to Biak on the north coast of New Guinea. From there we flew to the Wissel Lakes Missionary Station and were greeted by a group of missionaries—among them Darlene Deibler, who had remarried and was now Darlene Rose. We embraced and wept. Darlene whisked our one-year-old daughter into her arms. It was the first time she had met her namesake.

The Kapauku believers gathered around us and sang, "Jesus loves me, this I know." I had always thought of that song as a Sunday school chorus, but in that moment it became a hymn.

We lugged our supplies to the log house at Enarotali to live with the Roses. Although we were in a strange country, we felt as if we were home.

Lloyd and I plunged into language study, determined that God would give us the ability to converse in Kapauku. In three months we were asked to move ten miles southeast to Lake Tigi to begin a new mission station. A house had been built there, and we were preparing to move our belongings to the new site.

Our new home needed a lot of finishing, and Lloyd worked feverishly preparing it, hoping that the children and I would soon join him. But without warning I was stricken with a strange disease.

Although Lloyd was only ten miles away, it would have taken eight hours to reach him on foot through the rugged terrain. So without his knowledge, I was flown to the hospital in Hollandia, accompanied by Darlene Rose. Burney and Darlene were left behind with another missionary couple until Lloyd returned to the mission base at Enarotali. He stayed there with our children for two weeks, receiving medical reports about me by radio.

The news, however, was not encouraging. My condition was deteriorating rapidly, and the only remedy was an operation. The diagnosis was peritonitis, an inflammation of the membrane that lines the abdominal cavity. Death could result within a few hours or days.

Lloyd left the children in the care of missionary friends and flew to join me before surgery.

The operating room had only a roof with screen around the sides to protect the patients from flies. Sheets of metal perhaps three feet high surrounded the outer sides of the primitive structure. The floor was rough concrete.

The recovery room was much like the operating room, with one important difference: it did not have screens to ward off the pestilent flies and mosquitos. The patients slept under mosquito netting. An armed guard stood next to the operating room.

By the time I was carried into the operating room I was convinced that my death was imminent. And as if to confirm my suspicions, I was told that a Catholic priest had just died on the operating table. I was next in line. They tied my arms and legs with a rope, and after I responded to the anesthetic, the procedure began. When I came to, a chicken was sitting at the foot of my bed.

After the operation the doctor reported that he had found a cyst on my ovary, and when asked if he removed it, he nonchalantly replied no. He had not completed the surgery, and he gave no valid reason for his obvious negligence. Later I was told that an acute infection set in because the instruments used by this Dutch doctor were not sterilized.

Through a reliable source, we learned astonishing information regarding the doctor who had so carelessly treated me. While in Holland he had been a German collaborator. He gave secret information to the Nazis to enable them to take over his country. His punishment for espionage was to be sent to New Guinea. That explained the presence of a police guard just outside the door of the operating room.

Within a month I was able to return to Enarotali, and our family was united once again. But we never did move to the new area at Lake Tigi. God had other plans.

The Christian and Missionary Alliance was making plans to enter the Baliem Valley, situated deep in the interior of New Guinea. Lost to civilization, it had 60,000 inhabitants who had never heard of Jesus Christ. The Danis, as they were called, were reputed to be ferocious cannibals. The valley, Shangri-La, was isolated by ominous mountains and rugged terrain.

At the Alliance Field Conference in 1953, we along with the Roses and Einar Mickelson were asked to assist in the Baliem project. We moved to Sentani, the logical location for the central headquarters of the Baliem project. There we began to study Malay, the trade language of the islands. Spiritually, I was in high gear, medically I was in low. I had never recuperated completely from the surgery, and the peritonitis flared once again. A doctor at Enarotali suggested that pregnancy might improve my condition. We were overjoyed when we discovered that I was expecting our third child. But our optimism was short-lived. I had a miscarriage.

Early in 1954 we chartered a business plane from Australia to fly over the interior. Despite my illness, I was able to join Lloyd and three other missionaries to survey the Baliem Valley tucked among the formidable mountains of the bushy interior. The floor of the valley is 5,300 feet above sea level, with mountains of ten to thirteen thousand feet surrounding it. Lush green interspersed by garden patches carpeted the valley. A river ran its length.

As we flew over the small villages, we could see the Danis with spears ten to fifteen feet long walking along the trails. Women and children dashed into their houses; pigs scurried through the gardens.

If Dr. and Mrs. Welch had been aboard that flight they would have been disappointed in me. The sight of the Danis for whom we had prayed so often triggered a long string of emotional outbursts. I was looking at my future home—the valley for which God had given us a special burden. Lloyd spent his time in the air bent over a paper bag.

Our prayer was, "Lord, please let us enter, quickly!" God, however, was not following our timetable.

Six weeks later Lloyd and Einar Mickelson would land on the Baliem River and make contact with these stone-age people. I did not realize that more than a year would pass before my feet would walk through the villages we had just seen.

14

The Challenge of Shangri-La

During Word War II, Douglas MacArthur was in charge of the Allied forces in the Pacific. He was anxious to construct an airbase in the interior of New Guinea to be used by the United States' forces in emergency flights. At that time the interior was still widely believed to be uninhabited and an ideal location for such a project. Thus the Baliem Valley had been rediscovered by the American army. Later two war correspondents dubbed it "Shangri-La," adding to its mystery.

The Christian and Missionary Alliance was planning to enter the valley, but how? Could missionaries trek through the dark, thick forests?

Sixty thousand stone-age people were isolated at least one hundred eighty miles from civilization. Those miles were crammed with formidable mountains, dense forest, and murky swampland. On two occasions missionaries joined groups to find out whether the valley could be reached on foot. For the sake of the gospel they were willing to risk their lives for what Rudyard Kipling wrote about, "Something lost behind the ranges, lost and waiting for you—go."

Those two expeditions proved that the only way a mission station could be established was by landing an aircraft on the Baliem River.

In 1953 the Alliance began to raise funds to rent a plane for the project. The main base of operation would be Hollandria. The missionaries chosen were Einar Mickelson, Jerry Rose, and Lloyd Van Stone. We were ecstatic! Lloyd and I would be among the first white people to enter. Arrangements were made to charter a Quantas plane, but the governor of New Guinea forbade the plane to enter his country. So the decision was made to purchase a twin-engine amphibious sea plane that would be able to land on the river. The aircraft, named *The Gospel Messenger,* arrived in New Guinea in February, 1954. At last a flight appeared imminent.

But one more obstacle arose. All three wives were experiencing physical difficulties. Einar Mickelson's wife had been forced to remain in the United States with a heart condition. Darlene Rose was pregnant and flew home when she became ill. Jerry returned later. My peritonitis flared up. Undoubtedly, we were special targets of satanic attack. Would we ever get to the Baliem?

As my health steadily declined, my weight dipped to ninety pounds. The doctor advised me to return to the United States. The Alliance graciously suggested that Lloyd return with me, but we decided against it. God had brought us here, and His work must go on. I preferred to stay and die in New Guinea. But Lloyd reminded me, "Honey, we must take responsibility for the children." We decided that I would return to Houston with Burney and Darlene, ages four and three. Lloyd would stay to enter the valley.

That final night before our flight we stayed in a motel. As we prepared for bed I heard Burney sobbing beside his cot. "What's wrong, honey?" I asked.

"Oh Mommy, I don't think me can stand it," he said, his blue eyes brimming with tears.

"Stand what, Burney?"

"I can't stand to leave me Daddy."

I couldn't stand it either, as we embraced and wept at the

airport. Lloyd and I thought we might never again meet on earth. We agreed to leave our children with our friends Bob and Jesse Sylvester after my death. As the plane taxied down the runway, I felt as if half of me were being ripped out. The children pressed their noses against the window, crying, "Daddy, Daddy." As the plane circled I saw Lloyd sobbing openly, unashamedly. I would have bailed out of that plane had I not been confident that we were obeying our Lord. Deep within I knew I could cast myself on Him and He would comfort us now as He always had in the past.

And so Einar and Lloyd were left alone to land in the middle of Dani territory. Although warned by Dutch officials not to enter, they could not turn back. Lloyd quoted an army axiom, "We have to go in. We don't have to come back." The target date, April 20, 1954, arrived not a moment too soon.

Lloyd awoke at 5:30, had devotions, and arrived at the Lewises' home for breakfast by 6:00. An hour later he, Einar, the plane's capable pilot Al Lewis, and co-pilot Ed Ulrich were in *The Gospel Messenger*. Along with them was a converted Kapauku family, Elisa and Ruth Gobai and their two-year-old daughter, Dorcas. This family was included so that the Danis would know that their white visitors were friendly. Besides, an all male group could be a sign of hostilities. Later the missionaries learned that the Danis had not recognized Ruth as a woman. Perhaps two-year-old Dorcas helped communicate an atmosphere of friendship.

By 7:10 A.M. the plane was in the air. Lloyd described his thoughts: *Is it a dream? Can this really be true? Are we at last in our field of service with a goal to work for? No more delays? No more hindrances? No more sicknesses? No more trouble with the plane? Can it really be possible that we are on our way?*

Both Einar and Lloyd believed that they might well be

giving their lives in this venture. They had signed an agreement with the government of New Guinea that if anything should go wrong, the missionaries were on their own. The government had washed its hands of all responsibility. Furthermore, they had given verbal assurance to pilot Al Lewis that all the passengers would immediately exit from the plane once it landed. Al feared that the plane might not be able to take off with the passengers aboard at the altitude of 5,300, at which they would be landing. So having put their hands to the plow, they could not turn back.

They flew over the river to check for hidden logs. Then they circled around and came in for the landing. Suddenly they were on the water. The three men jumped out and worked their way to the eastern bank of the river, until the co-pilot was able to jump ashore. The plane was tied to a tree. Lloyd and Einar, standing in the water up to their hips, unloaded the plane. Fifteen minutes later the plane was airborne once again. The little group of five was left alone in the wilderness.

The ground had to be cleared of the canelike grass that grows ten to fifteen feet tall. By noon they had cleared an area big enough to pitch an eight- by eight-foot tent. That afternoon Einar and Elisa left camp for an hour and a half, trying in vain to reach an area about a quarter of a mile away that seemed suitable for drops by the plane. It was swampland and filled with mosquitos.

The party lunched on a can of Australian casserole steak (a fancy name that covers a multitude of sins), along with a can of date bread sent for Einar's birthday.

Lloyd describes the rest of the day: "That afternoon we continued clearing the brush from the river front so that the plane could come in safely the next day. Then a path was made to string up the one-hundred-foot radio aerial.

"For supper we had a can of cheese and a big pot of hot chocolate. Elisa, Ruth, and Dorcas were in the pup tent;

Einar and I in the umbrella tent. What an invasion party! But it is 'not by might, nor by power, but by my spirit, saith the Lord.' "

After years of planning, praying, and working, missionaries had arrived in Shangri-La. So far, there was no sign of a Dani.

Early the next morning Al Lewis made a second flight, bringing in linguist Myron Bromley, plus two Kapauku helpers who would assist in establishing the camp. He also brought a rubber boat loaned by the Dutch navy.

Then the excitement began! As soon as the plane took off, Elisa called to the other men. On top of a mountain, silhouetted against the sky, was a long line of Dani warriors, standing erect and holding fifteen-foot spears aloft like so many palings in a picket fence.

A more immediate problem was facing the missionaries. They needed to find a new location for a campsite. The water was rising, and their present location would soon be inundated. Directly across the river was a high mound that appeared more suitable. They went across to inspect it more closely. When they looked back across the river at their original campsite, they could hear the yells of a band of Danis inspecting the supplies. The men could not return easily, so they could only hope that the Danis would not tamper with their equipment.

While they were working feverishly to establish a new camp, two Danis appeared. All they wore were gourds. Both of them had long spears, which they propped against a tree; they had come to greet the missionaries.

Lloyd had just loaded his movie camera, so the meeting was captured on color film. Later, detailed pictures were taken of the Danis as they participated in their tribal customs. Anthropologists, interested in studying Dani culture, viewed the films with interest when we returned on furlough. Lowell Thomas interviewed Lloyd and provided opportunities for him to speak about his contact with these primitive tribes.

Lloyd wrote in his diary, "The Danis greeted us by shaking hands and putting their arms around us, giving us a gentle hug. They were covered with pig grease, and by the time we had been properly greeted, we were too! I had always heard that when God calls He enables, but I never experienced it until this moment. I loved those two men!

"Our first visitor took the pig tusk he had in his nose and showed me how it is placed into the hole of the nostril. I examined his spear, hoping he knew by the smile on my face that I wanted to be friendly and really admired his weapon. One of the men climbed up a tree and began watching the mountain slopes behind our camp. He kept saying, 'Selimike'; later we learned it meant 'enemy.'

"A large number, perhaps twenty-five, had by now assembled in our camp. Some wore fur headdresses with feathers sticking around the edges. One had a mop of hair that hung in literally hundreds of ringlets. Twenty or thirty stayed around the rest of the day and were trying to learn new words."

In answer to the prayers of hundreds of believers around the world, missionaries had made contact with the people in the Baliem Valley.

Two months after my arrival in the United States I was lying in the Herman Hospital in Houston recuperating from surgery. Jesse Sylvester walked into my room and asked, "Dorie, what is the best news that you would like to hear today?"

Without a pause I answered, "That the missionaries have made it into the valley."

"Look at this, Dorie!" A cable had been sent from Alliance headquarters in New York, saying that radio contact had been established with the missionaries in the Baliem Valley! All was well.

I cried. At long last the dream of many years had come true. Lloyd was home in the valley. Ten months would pass before the children and I could join him, but a beginning had been made.

15

Living in the Valley

The missionaries' entrance into the Baliem Valley became national news in the United States. Lowell Thomas carried the story on radio, stating that the "Baliem Valley was one of the last areas on earth to be touched by civilization and the Christian gospel."

The Danis were friendly to their visitors. But during the first few weeks the missionaries witnessed numerous battles among the tribes. On several occasions Danis were killed just outside the new campsite. The missionaries were puzzled about why the battles were taking place in the area they had chosen. Later they learned the answer: they had established camp in no-man's-land, a strip of land between two warring tribes! Thankfully, God spared their lives. Bit by bit Bromley was able to make strides in learning the language. For now, all was well.

In November, 1954, the children and I left New York on the ship *Orchides* and arrived nearly three months later in Sydney, Australia. Lloyd met us. What a glorious reunion! Burney leaped into his father's arms, but four-year-old Darlene did not recognize him.

Eleven months earlier, I had left for the United States thinking that my ministry with Lloyd in New Guinea was ended. Now I was returning in relatively good health, with a new home awaiting me in the valley.

Six-year-old Burney was apprehensive about seeing the Danis. "I'm afraid I'm going to be afraid to see them," he confided, not trying to conceal his anxiety. But his fear was replaced with pride when Al Lewis let Burney sit with him in the front seat of the plane. He sat tall and straight, holding the wheel for the forty-five-minute flight.

Thus on February 20, 1955, the children and I entered the valley with Lloyd. The plane splashed into the water and came to a halt on the Baliem River. We deplaned into a wooden flat-bottom boat and headed for shore. There at least fifty men and boys crowded around us, trying to touch the wife of Tuan Van Stone. I was the second white woman that they had seen. Darlene Rose had visited the valley a few months before.

They pinched me, put their greasy arms around me, and ran their hands up and down my legs. They pulled down my eyelids with their long, dirty fingernails. Their intentions were harmless—they only wanted to touch Mama Van Stone, but in their enthusiasm I was slightly injured. Lloyd came through with this advice, shouting above the commotion: "Yell, 'Heki Hakeke Hu.'"

"What does that mean?" I shouted back.

"Never mind, just say it." So I did. It worked. The Danis kept their distance. Later Lloyd told me that the words meant, "You can look, but do not touch!"

As those filthy Danis hugged me, I loved them. Our one request to the Lord had been to give us love. I'm no great linguist. But I can love people. And I loved those Danis.

We lugged our belongings to the house (about ten feet by twenty-five feet) we called home. Posts separated the two "rooms." This area of the valley was known as "Hetigema."

The Danis crowded around to watch our every move. Heads appeared through our screenless windows. They watched us eat, were fascinated by the way we washed ourselves, and were ecstatic when we brushed our teeth. They thought toothpaste was bird droppings. Darlene's doll that

Unpacking our supplies—always a source of interest to the Danis. It took so much for us to live, and so little for them!
(1955)

said "mama" caused a small stir: grown men ran away in amazement and later gained enough confidence to turn it over, bewildered by this strange child. They tried to determine whether it was male or female, and, having discovered it was neuter, concluded it was a spirit! When I put the doll in the window, it became a popular sideshow.

Since our house was a refuge for rats, we decided to have two cats flown in to help us win the battle. The cats had plenty to eat; indeed a few months later they looked like stuffed animals. The Danis had never seen cats before and wouldn't touch them. But when I handed the kitten to one man he looked carefully into its face and then put the kitten's head into his mouth! I thought he was going to bite it off. He proceeded to lick the kitten like a lollipop from head to tail. The kitten began to purr, and the Dani shouted, "Aniwu" (thunder), a word they had also used to refer to the airplane. They had never heard such a strange noise from an animal.

When one of the cats became sick, I asked Elisa to kill it. Shortly after that a warrior walked in sporting a new gray fur headdress. When I asked him where he got it, he told me he had seen Elisa kill the cat and watched where he buried it. In the night he dug it up, ate it, and saved its fur. "No one," he said, grinning broadly, "has a headdress like mine!"

The Danis were amazed at the sensation they received when they put their hands in a bucket of heated water. It had never occurred to them that they could heat water on a fire. When they saw a clothes wringer, they put sticks in it to see what would happen.

During a pig feast they kill as many as a dozen pigs and eat the meat for weeks after. When I was given a spoiled piece of pork as a gift and threw it out, they were surprised, thinking I had simply misplaced it. They brought it back into the house twice. The third time I buried it!

The Danis were amused by our strange behavior. Lloyd discovered that when he took his shoes off, they tapped their gourds and, putting their index fingers in their mouths, plucked their cheeks in amazement. On one trip to the village, Lloyd obediently removed his shoes and socks five times! In time he learned the reason for their astonishment: they believed that the white man was actually removing part of his anatomy!

Other items also caused a sensation. One Dani glanced into a mirror, then looked beyond it to see the man who stood in front of him whom he'd never met before! Another looked into a mirror and caught the image of a friend who stood behind him. He was incredulous. How could his friend be behind him and in front of him at the same time? Apparently he had only seen the man's spirit, he thought. Razor blades, cameras, and note pads provided more amusement. They rubbed the missionaries' arms to see if the whiteness would come off.

We had heard that the Danis were cannibals. As we lived among them we discovered they were, but they were cannibals with discrimination. They would cook and eat an enemy only if he were not too rich or too poor, too good or too bad. By every standard, they were primitive. They left human dung at the sides of their pathways. They had no smoke signals or drums. They made no paddles for their canoes but primitively navigated with poles.

The Danis never take a bath from birth to death. They cake themselves with pig grease, rub charcoal on their bodies, and cover themselves with mud during periods of mourning. Understandably, one need not be able to see in order to know that a Dani is near!

Yet odors are, after all, a matter of personal preference. Friday evenings, Lloyd and I agreed, would be our special evenings together. We would wash, put on clean clothes, and go for an evening stroll or play games with the children. To add a romantic touch, I brought a bottle of perfume with me into the camp. When I put some on, the Danis would exclaim, "Mama Van Stone, you stink!"

I have often been asked, "Doris, how could you really love those people?" Because I had experienced God's grace, I could give His grace. The Danis had no word for love; I had not known love until God loved me. The Danis often clubbed each other or beat their children until their eyes rolled back into their heads. I had been beaten. Throughout my childhood God had laid the foundation that allowed me to identify with the Danis. I understood their suffering and loved them.

The God I met back in the orphanage seemed to say, *Dorie, you were like one of them—rejected and ugly. But I loved you and transformed you. I can also transform them.*

My heart was broken when I witnessed the cruel tribal customs. For example, if a woman committed adultery, an arrow was put through her thigh. Frequently, children would have the tips of their ears cut off as a sign of mourning the death of a relative. Equally common was the practice of cutting off the tips of the fingers to show genuine sorrow at the time of a funeral.

Worse than the physical pain that these crude tribes inflicted upon themselves was their insensitivity to each other. With such feelings I could readily identify. I remembered my hurts.

No matter how obnoxiously they acted, we always befriended them. Once a Dani man watched carefully while I washed dishes. "Mama, I can do that," he offered. He put his hands in the hot water, and grease began to float toward the outside of the pan.

"No, I'll wash," I suggested, hoping that he would not object. Then he asked for a towel, insisting that he dry the dishes. He took it, held it firmly in his hands, tasted it, flipped it, and used it to rub the pig grease from his body. Gently, I assured him that I would *both* wash and dry the dishes.

One day I had the privilege of being initiated into a Dani tribe. Lloyd had had a similar experience in a different tribe shortly after he entered the valley. For me, it was the high point of our life in the Baliem.

It began with the chief shooting a pig with an arrow behind its right front leg. One of the men caught the blood in a banana leaf. Another Dani cut off a piece of fat, rubbed it in his hands, mingled it with blood and began to smear it on my head, face, hair, and legs. He put his finger on his nose, then on my nose, and said, "Mama, we are one. You can go into our villages and visit our people, and no harm will come to you."

I was thrilled! *Lord,* I prayed, *if I only had the words to explain to these people that it is not the blood of a pig that makes us one, but the blood of Jesus Christ!*

Our children also were accepted into Dani culture. The Danis made Darlene a little net to wear on her head and carry her dolls, just like Dani women carried their babies. They made Burney a miniature bow and arrow and taught him to hunt birds in the tall grass. He and his Dani playmates would roll rattan hoops down a hill, carefully aiming a stick through the rolling hoop, as they practiced for throwing a spear.

We often became discouraged, however. People around us were dying without knowing Christ as Savior. The first man to whom Lloyd gave a penicillin injection back in 1954 was Hawula. He had a severe case of yaws, a tribal disease that eats away the tissue and causes disfigurement. Two weeks later when Lloyd visited the same area, the man embraced him and showed him the newly healed spot where the disease had been. Lloyd became known as the man with the "Jesus needle."

So a friendship with Hawula grew out of our medical treatment. He soon became a traveling companion and close Dani friend. Lloyd loved that man and believed that he was possibly the key in opening the gospel to these people. Hawula also had the potential of becoming a language informant and a leader among his people.

Our second Christmas in the valley marked the first time we were able to share the Christmas story with the Danis. A few days before Christmas Lloyd and I, Burney and Darlene, and Myron Bromley went down into Magic Valley to

Dani man with disfiguring yaws. When Lloyd stopped the progression of the disease with an injection of penicillin, he became known as "the man with the Jesus needle."
(1958)

tell the people the story of the Nativity. When we arrived at the first village, the children sat down in the shade of a banana tree to escape the heat of the blazing sun. The Danis that gathered around us seemed upset, and a ripple went through the people. We could see they were paying attention to Burney and Darlene and motioning toward them. Lloyd went over to the children and told them to stand up. We saw that they had been sitting on human bones.

Immediately, Lloyd began questioning the people. When he asked whose bones they were, no one would answer. Later we learned that the Danis do not like to repeat the names of the dead lest the spirit of the dead one return to haunt them.

The people began whispering back and forth to each other, still refusing to give Lloyd the name of the dead person. He insisted, however, and after a while the chief whispered in his ear, "They're Hawula's bones." Hawula had been killed in a battle by the men of Olokoma, a tribe from the south. After his death the men of Olokoma returned his body to the Pugima tribe, where he was cremated. Only his bones remained—under the banana tree.

We were shocked. Lloyd froze in his steps. Hawula was dead. Lloyd says, "All that flashed through my mind was a missionary hymn that I had heard young people sing when I was in school:

> A hundred thousand souls a day
> Are passing one by one away,
> In Christless guilt and gloom
> Without one ray of hope or light
> With a future dark as an endless night,
> They are passing to their doom.

Lord, how could it be that this man just passed right through our fingers into eternity without Christ, and we didn't have the message in time to share it with him?

Our hearts were burdened, and we couldn't get an answer from heaven as to why our friend had slipped away before we could tell him the Good News. But he had.

16

Our Times Are in Thy Hands

We developed confidence in the Danis. Our children played with the Dani children and picked up the language rapidly. We were convinced that the Danis were not dangerous as had been suspected. Despite their tribal wars, we believed they would never hurt *us*.

We were wrong. On six occasions Lloyd's life was in danger; only the protection of God kept him from death.

One such occasion began innocently enough while we were working on our permanent house. Often Danis would come to help. One morning three teenage girls appeared at the camp. Although we didn't know from which village they had come, we let them work. At noon a heavy downpour halted the work; however, later we were able to do some work outside. They helped us until three o'clock in the afternoon. We paid them and sent them home, not realizing they were planning to cross a swollen stream.

At six-thirty that evening a young warrior came to our camp and asked if we knew the whereabouts of the girls. We explained that they had left, and he then told us that they had not returned to their village. It was feared they had drowned.

The next morning our camp was silent; no one came to visit us. That was a sure sign that something unusual had happened. Off to the east we could see people moving along the trail, but they took the long way around, avoiding our camp.

Elisa hesitantly walked down the trail to ask what was wrong. The news was stunning: the people were traveling east to attend the funeral of the three girls that had drowned. The body of only one girl had been found; the other two were swept away by the rapid current. We were deeply hurt and felt that God had let us down by allowing such a tragedy to happen. Would we be blamed?

Lloyd was reluctant to attend the funeral, knowing that his life could be in jeopardy. But he also knew that staying home would not solve the problem. Perhaps by attending he could demonstrate our sorrow. He and Elisa decided to go while Ruth and I stayed with the children.

The two men could hear the funeral dirge as they approached the village. Inside the fence a man sat alone on the ground, weeping. From inside the men's clubhouse, one lonely voice cried out the awful details while other men joined in a uniform chant.

In the village yard other men picked up stones and beat them against their heads until they drew blood. Then they burst out in loud weeping and wailing.

Lloyd gave gifts to the father of the girl whose body had been found. One man said, "Van Stone has a heavy heart, too. He's crying."

In the midst of their mourning someone called Lloyd to doctor a sick man. To his surprise it was the young warrior who had asked about the girls the night before. Suddenly, it became clear to him what had happened: this young man was engaged to one of the dead girls. To display his grief, he had cut off some of his fingers. Lloyd doctored the man's wounds as best he could, his heart broken over the cruel suffering these people inflicted upon themselves.

A large group of men began to gather in the village yard, staring intently at Lloyd and Elisa. Tension was mounting; silence hung like a cloud over the village.

Lloyd wanted to run, but he knew that was unwise. He

spoke to Elisa as casually as possible and suggested they return to Hetigima. They left the village, trying to act nonchalant. They prayed as they walked, knowing that they could not run until they were out of sight. Finally, they got to the river, crossed it hurriedly, and ran all the way home. Ruth and I thanked God that our men had returned safely.

Early the next morning, Yamke, the brother of Chief Ukumhearik, pounded on our door, demanding that Lloyd come to help the chief. Lloyd felt he had to go—in case the chief was really sick; he took the medicine kit and his pistol. Another man had awakened Elisa and was insisting that he come, too. With both men gone, Ruth and I would be left alone with the children. What could it all mean?

As Lloyd and Elisa arrived at the chief's house, Dani men from many villages were gathering inside the long house. Chief Ukumhearik took his place across from Lloyd. Then a solemn ceremony took place. The witch doctor began chanting; soon everyone in the room joined him. They were beseeching the evil spirits to depart from the gifts from Lloyd to the dead girl's father.

A speech followed: "Van Stone, before you came to the Baliem we were poor; we didn't have cowrie shells and razor blades, mirrors or axes, nor did we have medicine. You brought us all those things, and you are good.

"But, Tuan Van Stone, yesterday at the funeral the young men blamed you for the death of the three girls. They were planning to kill you as you left the village. But as you were leaving, Chief Ukumhearik arrived and stopped them from killing you. They had informed the chief of their plans, and he ran to the village to stop them!"

Lloyd said he thought his heart had stopped beating, but the pounding in his ears assured him it had not. Chief Ukumhearik spoke to Lloyd, explaining that it had been our kindness to his brother Hutunsek that had caused him to intervene and save Lloyd's life. Hutunsek had broken his leg, and Lloyd had spent six weeks with him on the coast until his leg healed. Now Lloyd sat in the midst of these men who had wanted to kill him yesterday, praising God for sparing his life.

Two hours had passed since Lloyd and Elisa had left. We waited anxiously, not knowing what was happening. Suddenly, we heard the noise of a plane circling overhead. Ruth and I ran outside and frantically waved at the pilot. Because of difficulty in radio connections, our friends on the coast had not heard from us for five days; they thought all of us had been murdered. In fact, the pilot had strict orders not to land unless someone came out of the camp and waved.

Not long after the plane landed, Lloyd and Elisa returned and shared what had taken place. Lloyd was pale—obviously shaken by the realization that he had narrowly escaped a death plot.

That evening we prayed to God with much thanksgiving. It was He who had led Lloyd to help Hutunsek and win the boy's respect and friendship. In turn, it was that kindness that God used to move the heart of Chief Ukumhearik to prevent Lloyd's death.

Several months later, Lloyd had an even closer brush with death. One morning Dick Lanehan, Jerry Rose, and Lloyd decided to investigate a new area of the valley in a prefabricated, plywood motor boat that had been flown in. They were anxious to follow a stream that emptied into the Baliem. As they traveled west, they came to a tree that had fallen across the river and now was used for a bridge. The three climbed out of the boat and pulled it over the log. Just on the other side, a group of Danis were hiding in the bushes.

The missionaries greeted them warmly, then tied their boat to a huge tree that supported a lookout platform. They knew they were in no-man's-land; during the day a man would often be on the platform looking for the enemy. Jerry stayed with the boat while Lloyd and Dick walked to the village a few hundred yards away. This tribe of Danis had no doubt heard of the "Jesus needle," for some of them who had yaws indicated that they wanted a shot of penicillin. Lloyd began treating the people, when suddenly, without warning, an old man stepped out of the bush thirty feet away, and walked defiantly toward Lloyd and Dick. His spear was poised as he hissed "Pugima selimike," which means "the enemy from Pugima." The missionaries were identified with their enemies!

Lloyd tells what happened: "Instantly all the men turned to run inside the village to grab their spears, which were propped against a fence or nearby tree. The women and children vanished. The men circled us with spears raised and arrows pointing toward us. I tried to talk to the man who had started it all, but my voice could not be heard above the yelling. One man tried to say a few words to the old man on our behalf, but he was brushed aside. Just as they were ready to throw their spears, I fired my pistol into the air. The shot was deafening and so was the silence that followed. The men slowly put their weapons down, looking in every direction to figure out where the noise had originated. I wanted to run but before I did, I put the medicine back into the kit, closed it, and then dashed toward the river.

"Dick led the way racing down the trail toward the boat. We jumped down the embankment, and ran around the mudhole. Glancing over my shoulder, I saw a Dani throw his spear. I stepped sideways as it whizzed past me, shoulder high. It stuck in the mud beside me, quivering. I froze momentarily, then continued toward the boat. Dick hopped in first; I followed on his heels. Jerry was firing his gun into the air to keep the Danis back, but since the shots did no damage the men kept running toward us.

"Frantically, I began to unwind the cable I had wrapped around the tree less than an hour before. I couldn't believe I had wound it around so many times! The air was alive with spears and arrows. As soon as the cable was released, Jerry started the motor and we scooted around the narrow neck of land at breakneck speed. Then, we saw the serious dilemma that faced us. The Danis were running swiftly and would beat us to the log that crossed the river! We didn't have time to discuss our strategy. Dick jumped onto the bank of the narrow river, firing his gun into the air. Jerry hopped on one side of the log, I on the other. We lifted the boat and pulled. What had been a difficult and cumbersome project an hour before was now accomplished with dispatch and ease. In fact, the boat seemed as light as a feather. As we pushed it over the log, I noticed that a branch was in my way; I broke it off. As soon as the boat was over the log I jumped in, inexplicably tripping and nearly falling on my face.

"Back in the boat I looked down and saw that the branch I had broken was actually an arrow that had gone into the upper part of my leg, and the end was sticking out. It was the arrow and not a branch that had caused me to stumble.

"Dick jumped into the boat, and we took off again. The warriors kept coming but eventually had to give up chase since the trails no longer continued along the river."

The men dared not stop. In and out, under limbs and around stumps they sped. When they reached the Baliem River, they stopped to pray, thanking God for the deliverance of the past hour. By the time they arrived at the camp, Lloyd's leg was hurting badly. He put a poncho around his body, covering his legs so that the Danis at our camp would not know that he had been shot with an arrow.

Hearing the commotion outside, Darlene Rose and I ran out to greet the men, not knowing that one of them was injured. I realized that Lloyd was limping, and then to my horror I saw the arrow sticking out of his swollen leg. Jerry Rose performed a minor operation on Lloyd. First, he took a razor and enlarged the opening of the wound. Then he carefully pulled the arrow out with a pair of pliers. However, a strip of orchid fiber, used on the tip of an arrow to cause a quick infection, was still embedded beneath the skin. Jerry used tweezers to remove the last piece, and then thoroughly cleansed the wound. The treatment ended with Lloyd getting some of his own medicine—a shot of penicillin.

It was now early afternoon. For about an hour all of us sat around discussing what had happened and what had gone wrong. We were amazed that no one had been killed. How we praised and thanked God that He had spared Jerry's, Dick's, and Lloyd's lives.

Our rejoicing was to be short-lived. God did not choose to spare the life of one of our fellow missionaries.

Early that same morning pilot Al Lewis had radioed us for weather conditions. We reported that the sky was overcast, and we discouraged him from making a flight into the valley.

We had just concluded our discussion over the men's narrow escape when we heard a plane circling overhead. We were surprised because we had assumed that Al had canceled his flight that day because of the bad weather. It was also unusual for a plane to come in the afternoon; the normal procedure was for morning flights.

Jerry and Dick rushed outside and saw that it was a government plane. As it passed over for the third time it dropped a message, "Radio Sentani immediately. Emergency."

Jerry and Dick left on the run to make radio contact. The battery on the radio was so low, however, that the people at Sentani were unable to hear Jerry and Dick. But the men could hear Mary Lewis, Al's wife, and Myron

Bromley trying to make contact with Al by radio. *Oh, no! Al Lewis had attempted a flight into the valley but had not arrived!*

That night we slept in fear. What had happened to Al and the plane? What would be the future of the work in the Baliem if the plane and its pilot was lost? We were restless and anxious.

The next day we learned that Al had reported his last position over the Idenburg River at 9:23 A.M. Apparently, dark clouds had closed in on him as he sought to guide the plane through the treacherous pass to the valley.

That afternoon the Dutch government started an aerial search that continued for the next five days. MAF pilots flew back and forth across the high ridges, seeking to locate the amphibian and its pilot.

Exactly four weeks after Lewis had left the Sentani airstrip, the wreckage of his plane was spotted. News of the crash overwhelmed our wounded spirits. Fear flooded our grieving hearts. We had always known that our stay in the Baliem involved risks. But now Al Lewis was dead and we were without a plane. The future of our missionary work hung in the balance.

On top of all that, Lloyd had been shot with a Dani arrow. We had come to believe that the tales regarding the Danis' savagery had been exaggerated. Yet we had had numerous threats made against us, and the latest episode confirmed our fear that we could be killed at any time.

A few days after the crash, the governor of New Guinea ordered that all women and children be evacuated from the Baliem and be flown to the coast on a government plane. Darlene and I and our children said good-bye to our husbands and left for Sentani.

Lloyd and Jerry told us later that they wept uncontrollably after we left. The emotions they had been hiding from us spilled out. They believed they might never see us again.

An uncanny fear gripped Lloyd and intensified day by day. Sleeping alone in the house one night, he heard someone outside slap the aluminum corrugated sheeting. Only at sunrise did Lloyd finally fall asleep.

To overcome his fear, Lloyd forced himself to go into the villages to doctor the sick. Each time he had to battle an overwhelming force that told him not to go, but he went hoping that his actions would overcome the fear.

One evening the showdown came: either he had to conquer his fear or be conquered by it. Lloyd walked up and down beside a stone fence at the back of the property. He could no longer pray; his words seemed to be mockery. The anguish was now so overpowering that all he could do was plead the blood of Christ. The Scripture says Satan is overcome by the blood of the Lamb. From that moment on, Lloyd's fear began to leave. The source of his fear had been identified—Satan. The way to victory was clear—the triumph of Christ at the cross. Even when Lloyd returned to the village where he had been shot, his fear did not hinder him.

Although the wreckage of the plane Al had flown was spotted high on the rugged slopes of the north side of a cliff, the Dutch government concluded that it had neither the manpower nor the equipment to organize an overland search party. Later three separate expeditions would be undertaken to get to the plane. On the second, Lloyd accompanied government officials and a group of carriers, in a determined effort to reach the crash site. They were gone one week, and had to return because their food supply was gone.

Four years after the crash, a third party did reach the plane. They discovered that the two previous expeditions were within a few hundred feet of the crash. Al's body had evidently almost broken in two on impact. The small group of men held a brief funeral service in memory of the courageous pilot.

The work in the Baliem Valley had to continue. Although we were discouraged and grief stricken, Al Lewis's memory spurred us on.

17

Promise You'll Bury Me

Before the children and I could return to the valley, the government required that an airstrip be built. No longer could planes land on the unpredictable Baliem River. To the east lay a long slope running parallel to the Aigaik River. It was covered by boulders, stone fences, abandoned gardens, and trees. But it was the only suitable location. Without tools or modern equipment the ground would have to be cleared and prepared for an airplane to land. The chief and witch doctor agreed that the project could begin. Word was sent to the villages asking that people come to help. They would be paid for their efforts.

Approximately forty people showed up each day for the job. More than a hundred trees were cut down and the roots burned out. Fourteen stone fences were dismantled and carried stone by stone to the side of the strip. In some places three or four feet of topsoil was dug up and carried to the side. Some stones and boulders were too big to move, so fires were built on top of them to burn them down layer by layer.

Each day from early morning until evening the work continued. Slowly the rugged terrain was being transformed into a long, smooth runway. In less than two months the airstrip at Hetigema was ready to receive its first airplane. In July 1955, Burney, Darlene, and I were reunited with Lloyd. I was glad to be back with my husband and in our valley home.

At home in Hetigema on Easter, 1956. The Dani boy pictured became friendly with Lloyd and stuck to him like a shadow.

Life returned to normal. For several months the Dani tribes were peaceful and friendly. Our fears subsided, and we felt confident that our friendship with the people at Hetigema would give us an opening to share the gospel with other Dani tribes.

Then, one afternoon, without warning, it seemed that my ministry in the valley would come to an abrupt end. I became very ill. My temperature shot up to 104 degrees, and I had an excruciating pain in my abdomen. We tried to radio Sentani, but there was static on the line, and we could not establish contact. That meant no medical help from the outside, no plane to take me to a doctor.

Lloyd, Burney, and Darlene prayed outside my room, wanting to avoid contact in case my sickness was contagious. But for one fleeting moment Darlene knelt beside my bed asking God to spare her mother.

I thought I was dying. And although I did not fear death, I was repulsed at the thought of cremation. Dani culture requires that a corpse be burned. So I asked Lloyd to promise that if I died, he would bury me. He assured me that my wish would be granted, and he even chose a spot: a mound of earth beside a tree, just behind the camp. There was no wood for a coffin, so he decided which part of the house he would tear down to build one. With those matters taken care of, I awaited my entrance into heaven.

Lloyd and I did not consider ourselves heroic. We had both come near to death on numerous occasions—I with my illness, and he being attacked by hostile Danis. But we were convinced that there was a price to be paid to bring the gospel to the Baliem Valley, and if death be a part of that price, so be it.

Lloyd sent Elisa to Dr. Bromley's house to see whether he had anything that might help. At midnight Lloyd prayed to God again for wisdom that he might know how to treat me. The thought occurred to him that he should put hot towels on my abdomen, and in the absence of any other possible remedy, he did that, and waited.

Later Elisa returned from Dr. Bromley's house to report that he had no medicine, but he sent along a few sheets of paper, giving remedies for various ailments. To Lloyd's surprise, on one paper were these words: "If the illness is hepatitis it is hard to identify it in the first stages. The skin doesn't turn yellow until a few days later. If pain is intense in the upper part of the abdomen, place hot dry towels on the area until relief comes."

On each successive day I grew weaker. We had not had radio contact for six days, so that the possibility of help was remote. Then one morning we heard the sound of the plane in the distance, but the pilot did not land immediately. He had been told to fly over the camp, and if no one waved, he was to assume we had been martyred. When he saw signs of life, he landed.

Lloyd made a stretcher and with the help of Elisa carried me to the airstrip. Burney and Darlene were outside the house when I left, and I could not find them to say good-bye. After I left, Lloyd found them kneeling beside a stone fence praying for their mother.

Eight weeks passed while I convalesced in Hollandia. When I returned to the valley, Chief Ukumhearik was on hand for my arrival. He pushed Lloyd aside and gave me a bear hug. While I was gone he had used Lloyd's typewriter, pressing a handful of keys simultaneously, to send me a message. Although the paper he had sent with Lloyd's letter contained nothing but gobbledygook, he wondered whether I understood his message. "Of course, I did," I assured him. "You wanted Mama Van Stone to get well."

"That's it! That's it! You understood it," he exclaimed, beaming from ear to ear.

Repeatedly, I thanked our Lord that Lloyd did not have to bury me on the mound behind our camp.

After we had completed our first term we returned to the United States for our furlough. The churches that had supported us greeted us warmly. Lloyd was interviewed by Lowell Thomas and gave numerous lectures sponsored by the Keedic Lecture Bureau. We were grateful that God had given us the privilege of making inroads into the one of the most primitive cultures in the world.

18

Mother, What Is a Memorial?

It was now 1959. Two years had passed since we took our furlough. We had been in New Guinea for seven years. Five of them had been spent with the Danis. The brilliant linguist Myron Bromley had made great strides in understanding the Dani language and culture. Other missionaries had joined us. As far as we knew, we would continue working there for years.

But one morning we received an urgent message in the valley. The headquarters in Sentani radioed, "Lloyd go to the airstrip immediately—the pilot will have a message for you."

Burney and Darlene were in the new missionary school that had been established in Sentani. The message *had* to be about them. Since all our radio calls were monitored, it was customary not to communicate tragic news via radio. Now all we could do was wait. *O God, what is it?*

Lloyd and I waited anxiously at the airstrip. As soon as the plane landed and taxied close to us, the pilot called out of the window, "It's Burney." The roar of the plane's engine faded into silence. "Burney is missing. Darlene knows nothing of his whereabouts—he's run away!"

Something within us died. Lloyd's knees buckled; he held onto the plane to steady himself. Frightful thoughts flooded our minds. *Burney? Run away?* The school at Sentani was near an undeveloped land area; the trails were hazardous, and snakes were often seen in the underbrush.

What would have made a nine-year-old boy run away at night? Where could he be? Burney was afraid of the dark. In fact, he wouldn't go into a dark room unless he pushed Darlene in ahead of him. For years she thought he was just being polite.

With a hurried kiss and words of reassurance, Lloyd said good-bye and jumped into the plane to fly back with the pilot. Slowly, I walked back to our house crying aloud. In a few moments Darlene Rose came over, and together we threw ourselves at the Lord. *God, You know where Burney is. You've got to help them find him!*

In retrospect, we should have known that Burney might buckle under the tension of leaving us in the valley to go to school in Sentani. He and Darlene had adjusted well to life in the Baliem; they learned the Dani language, played with the other children, and understood the Dani's strange customs. But at age nine Burney also knew the dangers of living in the valley. He was with us when Lloyd was attacked and when our lives were threatened on several occasions. He had even told us that he believed that we, his parents, would die in the Baliem. He had often expressed his concern for us.

During our first term in the valley I had taught both the children. But when we returned after our first furlough, Burney, nine, and Darlene, eight, attended the missionary children's school at Sentani. From the beginning Burney had fought this requirement. He vowed he would never leave us. When we *forced* him to stay at the school, he was terrified. His concern for our safety had turned into worry and fear, a terrible burden for a nine-year-old boy.

As we saw it, however, we had no alternative. In accepting the missionary call, we had realized we would have to sacrifice. We also believed we must be totally obedient to the mission society. That meant Burney and Darlene *had* to go to school one hundred eighty miles away from their home, or we would have to return to the United States.

Now the hours dragged on as Darlene Rose and I waited for a message from the coast. Again and again I visualized the worst: perhaps he would not be found, or if found he would be dead. *O God, You can't—*

Finally, just before noon, Lloyd's voice came over the radio, "Doris, Burney has been found—he is fine—I'll explain later."

Late that afternoon Lloyd returned to the valley with Burney and Darlene. At the airstrip we hugged and wept, relieved to know that God had brought us together again.

Bit by bit, I learned what had happened. The night before, Burney had gone to his sister's room after the lights were out.

"Darlene, I've got to get to Mom and Dad in the valley. They need me—I'm going to run away!"

"Burney, you can't—"

"I've got to. I understand the language, and if the Danis were to plan an attack I could save Dad and Mom. Don't you see? Darlene, please promise not to tell anyone. Please?"

"I promise."

She kept her word. Burney quietly slipped out of the residence and walked along the dark path to the open hangar where the plane was kept. Childish imagination had his escape into the valley all planned: he would hide in the plane, and when the pilot made the next flight, Burney would soon be back in the valley with his father and mother! He even wore two suits of clothes; he knew he would need some extra clothes but couldn't carry them in a suitcase.

Once in the hangar he groped his way to the plane, but to his disappointment the door was locked. He decided he would find a place to sleep, and in the morning would sneak into the plane while it was being loaded. By using a ladder that was leaning against the wall, Burney was able to climb onto a platform that formed the top of an office inside the hangar. Hiding behind some materials stored on the platform, he fell asleep.

Morning came, but Burney kept sleeping. Neither the pilot loading the plane nor the roar of its engine awakened him. But by the time Lloyd had flown in from the valley and arrived in Sentani at eleven o'clock, Burney was standing at the hangar with Jerry Rose at his side.

The teachers at the school suggested that he and Darlene be given a week in the valley with us, hoping Burney would ultimately adjust to attending school away from home. But at the end of the week Burney asked once again, "Do I *have* to go back?"

"If you don't, we can't stay on the field," I replied, hiding the deep hurt that I felt within. *Lord, give us wisdom to know what to do,* my heart cried out.

"Why don't we pray about it and find out what God wants?" I finally suggested.

The next morning Darlene came out of her bedroom with her suitcase packed and her hair combed. "What did you decide, dear?" I asked.

"I'm going back, Mommy," she replied. "But why does Jesus ask us to do such hard things?"

I couldn't answer my daughter. The tears came, and I wept bitterly. "I don't know. I guess He just wants us to," was all I could say.

Burney had not changed his mind; he refused to go back to the school. With heavy hearts, Lloyd and I *forced* Burney to return.

"Burney," I tried to explain. "Sometimes we have to do things, but we don't understand why. Mother and Daddy have to send you to school, or we can't stay in New Guinea.

We love you dearly, Burney, and whenever you need us, we'll come."

Burney still clung to me, and I had to pry him forcibly away. That was like pulling away a part of my life. Lloyd and I knew that such a decision could not be justified—how could we be separated from our children when they needed us most? How could we ask them to be away from us when they knew our lives were in danger? Surely God would not require that.

Yet paradoxically, we also knew that God had called us to the Baliem Valley. His will was unmistakable, direct, clear. It boiled down to this: either our children would go to the mission school in Sentani or we would have to return to the United States. *God, how can You expect us to make such a decision? Surely, Your will does not conflict.*

The children were flown back to Sentani and settled in school again. But Burney did not adjust. He would not eat, he did no schoolwork, and he even refused to speak. We decided that I should fly to Sentani to be with Burney for a few days. When I arrived he had been sobbing for two days.

"Burney, just tell me why you ran away. I won't spank you—tell Mommy."

"No—no—" he sobbed, flinging himself across the bed, too weak to speak.

The next day he again refused to eat, and his sobbing turned into weak grunts. Nor would he tell me why he ran away or what was bothering him. On the third day I was desperate. If he didn't begin to speak and eat soon we would have to leave immediately for the United States. Heartbroken, I prayed and wept, wondering how this nightmare would end. That afternoon Burney spoke.

"Mom-my, I-I wa-ant to ta-a-l-k to you," he stuttered. I sat with him on the bed and put my arm around him.

"Mom-my, wha-at's a mem-mori-al?" he asked.

"A memorial is something you build in the memory of someone who has died, so you won't forget him," I explained.

"Mom-my, tha-at's all Dar-lene and I will h-ave if I don't go ba-ack to the val-ley with you." He threw himself onto my lap, sobbing hysterically. "Plea-se don't ma-ake me lea-ve you—ever. I'll do any-thi-ing, any-thi-ing you ask. Just don't e-ver ask me to lea-ve you again."

Then it hit me. Burney felt just as I had felt when left at the orphanage—pushed aside and totally rejected. I couldn't force my child to endure such rejection.

"Burney," I assured him, "Mommy promises—we'll never ask you to leave us again—ever!"

An incident had taken place during our recent furlough that explained Burney's question to me. He had had a dog named Blondie. One day the dog ran into the street and was killed by a car. Burney's grandfather buried the dog in the backyard, and my son had put a stick on the little grave. It was a memorial to his pet. He thought that was all he would have left of his mother and father if they stayed in the valley without him.

After my promise that we would never leave him, Burney recovered from his fears. There was no position available for us in Sentani, so Lloyd and I began to make preparations to return to the United States.

I wanted with all my heart to win Danis. But my first responsibility was to win Burney and Darlene. God had used us as trailblazers in the Baliem. Someone else would reap the harvest. But we had a harvest to reap in our son and daughter.

Another serious problem had developed to the point that we couldn't ignore it any longer: my health. My weight had dropped to ninety pounds again. I was weak and exhausted. The doctor had told me that if I did not get proper medical attention soon, I would be buried in the Baliem.

Reluctantly, we faced the fact that our days as missionaries in the Baliem might soon be over. Unresolved conflicts churned within us. God had called us, yet now we had to return. I've often pondered Darlene's question, "Why does Jesus ask us to do such hard things?"

19

Good-bye to the Valley

The time for our departure had come.

We were struggling with two conflicting desires. Our hearts were in New Guinea, where God had called us; but our God-given parental responsibility and my ailing health were forcing us to return to the homeland.

We had been living at a new mission station at the far end of the valley when the time came for us to leave. On our flight out of the valley the pilot had promised that he would touch down at the airstrip at Hetigema where we had helped establish a mission station several years before. There we had lived and worked as a family. To us it was like coming home.

Hours earlier the pilot had radioed Hetigema, announcing that we would land there briefly. Word spread that we were coming. When the plane touched down, no one was there to greet us except Yamake, the brother of the chief. He told us that everyone was gathered in the village; pigs were being killed—they were planning to have a feast for us! They thought we would be able to stay with them for several hours. We were overwhelmed by their kindness but had to decline their hospitality. The pilot was insistent that we could not stay; we had to leave almost immediately.

Yamake embraced us, deeply regretting that we had to leave. Then he added, "Van Stone, we don't understand a thing you tell us, but if we ever understand, we'll let you know—we promise!" And with that we left.

The pilot circled the camp once more, giving us our last look at the village. Burney, quoting the question Darlene had asked on a previous occasion, said, "Mother, why does Jesus ask us to do such hard things?" We had given our lives to these people, and yet Lloyd and I did not have the privilege of leading one Dani to Jesus Christ. We were pioneers helping to open a door that others would walk through.

Back in the United States we settled in Houston, Texas. As my health improved, we began visiting the churches that had supported us, thanking the people for their prayers and financial gifts. We found that some believers could not understand why we had returned from the field. One woman met us at the church door after the meeting. "You've disappointed us. Why didn't you trust God for healing out there? He'd have taken care of you and your children."

I stood in the church lobby and wept. To some, missionary work conveys an aura of adventure and heroism. When you return home because of the harsh realities of life, they cannot understand. *Lord, please help me to remember I am not responsible to people but to You.*

However, there was much to encourage us. God had a plan for our lives in the United States. He began opening doors to a new ministry motivating others to consider committing themselves to Christ for missionary work.

A woman whose testimony appeared in *Power* magazine was converted through Lloyd's preaching. In part she wrote, "Chief Ukumhearik had once prevented his murderous tribespeople from killing Lloyd Van Stone, sparing him so that I was able to hear the truth about Christ's sacrifice of Himself for my sins. It was as if an arrow of conviction from the Baliem Valley had pierced my heart, thus opening the way for the Savior to make me whole."

Yes, God could use us back in the United States.

When our financial support was terminated by the mission, Lloyd became employed at the Ford Motor Company in Houston. He worked there for several years while ministering in various churches on the weekends.

In 1965 God directed us into full-time pastoral ministries. Although deeply absorbed in the burdens and opportunities of the ministry, we kept in close touch with the work continuing in the Baliem Valley. Linguists had gone in and were able to conquer the language barrier and grasp the meaning of the Dani culture. The gospel began to penetrate with clarity and power.

While living in the valley our son Burney had prayed regularly that his playmate Agalawe would accept Christ as Savior. After we had been in the United States for three years, Ben and Ruth Karcesky, missionaries from the Baliem, had a message for Burney. One day Agalawe had asked Ben to lean down so he could whisper something in his ear. "Tell Mama and Tuan Van Stone that we are beginning to believe," he said. As far as we know, Agalawe was the first Dani in the Baliem to accept Christ!

Yamake, who had sorrowfully bid us farewell at the airstrip, also is a believer today.

In 1975 the Roses visited the valley, and some of the people who remembered us asked about our welfare. "How come you remember them?" Darlene asked.

"Because they told us about Jesus Christ, just like you did," was their answer.

In September, 1976, we received a letter from a man in the Baliem who wanted to write to thank us for coming to visit him many years ago. Here is one sentence from that letter which we treasure: "I just want you to know that we are now one in Jesus Christ."

That God should have given us the privilege of helping in pioneer missionary work is an inexpressible honor. Whatever we accomplished is to His everlasting credit. We've never been able to get out from under the burden for

With Burney and Dani boy at Hetigema (1958). Burney prayed that this boy would be one of the first Danis to come to know Jesus. We learned after our return home that he did become a Christian.

the people of the Baliem, but we have continued to share that burden with others. At a recent missionary conference, someone asked, "How long has it been since you returned from New Guinea?"

"About fifteen years," I replied.

"I can't believe it! You talk as though you just arrived on the last plane!" was the surprised comment.

Whether we are in Denver, Minneapolis, or Chicago, Shangri-La is never far from our minds and hearts. We keep praying, *Lord, keep the fire in our hearts burning. Keep our call to New Guinea fresh so that we can share it with others.*

There is one event that for us cannot happen too soon, and that is our reunion with Dani believers at the throne of our Lord Jesus in heaven. We join with all the missionaries in the Baliem Valley in awaiting the day when the Scripture will be fulfilled:

> After this I beheld, and, lo, a great multitude, which no man could number, of all nations, and kindreds, and people, and tongues, stood before the throne, and before the Lamb, clothed with white robes, and palms in their hands; and cried with a loud voice, saying, Salvation to our God which sitteth upon the throne, and unto the Lamb.
>
> **Revelation 7:9-10**

20

Healing the Brokenhearted

I had been invited to show slides and share our work in the Baliem Valley with a group of women at a country club in Kansas. A woman in the audience leaned over and whispered to another, "What's this girl done—what's she got to say?"

"Oh, she's been a missionary."

"A missionary? Is that all?" With that, the woman decided to make her exit, but the room was so crowded she couldn't make it to the door. She was trapped. Like it or not, she'd have to listen to a missionary.

After the slides, I was asked to share briefly about how I became involved in missionary work. The woman who had wanted to leave listened to my story. She came to talk to me after the meeting. She was dejected, depressed, and frustrated. Within a few minutes she was ready to accept Christ as her Savior and give Him a chance in her life. Today she is grateful that she was not able to leave the ladies' meeting when she wanted to!

Experiences like that encouraged me. Since our missionary work in New Guinea had come to such an abrupt end, could it be that God would use us here in the United States? Lloyd and I have committed ourselves to the ministry of challenging young people to surrender their lives for missionary service around the world.

Whenever I share my life story, someone comes to me afterward. "Dorie, I know what you've been through. My parents hated me too." Then they blurt out a story of child abuse or rejection or perhaps tell me that they also were reared in an orphanage. Some have shared stories that make my life seem relatively happy. Scores have told me of the bitterness that erupted in their lives because their parents were divorced. Often children are farmed out to relatives, used as pawns in a bitter marital struggle, or otherwise abused.

Repeatedly God has shown me that my experience is to be used to help others work through the hurts of childhood. As Paul wrote, the God of all comfort "comforteth us in all our tribulation, that we may be able to comfort them which are in any trouble, by the comfort wherewith we ourselves are comforted of God" (2 Corinthians 1:4). I've often said that one aching heart knows when another heart is aching. My turbulent childhood enables me to say to others, "I *know* how you feel."

My many contacts with people have reaffirmed my conviction that the starting point in putting a shattered life back together is a personal relationship with Jesus Christ. After I shared my testimony at a women's rally, a woman invited me to her home. She wore an expensive dress and glittered with exquisite jewelry—necklaces, bracelets, and several diamond rings. I walked into her plush home and sat down with her on the elegant sofa. She began to cry. "Dorie, my husband is a famous manufacturer; now he's having an affair, and I'm a nervous wreck. I've been to doctors and psychiatrists, and now I'm on tranquilizers twenty-four hours a day. What can I do?"

"Ever try Jesus?"

"No."

I explained the gospel simply: Christ died to redeem us, and He is a specialist at healing broken hearts. A few moments later she made the same decision I made in the orphanage. She accepted God's forgiveness and gave herself completely to Christ.

One day she stopped by to see me. "Dorie, I'm broken-hearted. My husband divorced me—*but with Christ I can make it.*" With Christ, people caught in the web of bitterness and rejection can make it! One of my favorite passages of Scripture is recorded in Luke. Christ picked up the scroll and read a passage from Isaiah, "The Spirit of the Lord is upon me because he hath anointed me to preach the gospel to the poor; he hath sent me to heal the broken-hearted, to preach deliverance to the captives, and recovering of sight to the blind, to set at liberty them that are bruised" (Luke 4:18). Christ has ointment for the bruises and wounds of the soul.

I genuinely believe that God never lays more on us than we can bear. People have told me, "But, Dorie, if you only knew my background—" I'm impressed with the words of Scripture, "There hath no temptation taken you but such as is common to man: but God is faithful, who will not suffer you to be tempted above that ye are able; but will with the temptation also make a way to escape, that ye may be able to bear it" (1 Corinthians 10:13). There is no hardship or tragedy that has not already been faced successfully by someone else. That fact can be comforting. No human being's situation is totally unique; no person can say, "I'm alone in my grief, no one has ever faced this before." Christ, the Great Physician, has already treated countless people whose problems are more severe than yours or mine.

The next step in putting the pieces of a broken life together is to forgive those who have wronged you. One question I'm constantly asked is, "Dorie, aren't you bitter toward your mother?" My reply is no I am not. As a child in the orphanage and during the difficult years that followed I experienced periods of bitterness. But I *chose* to forgive my mother even though I knew she would never respond to me.

Perhaps the most basic mistake made by those who are bitter is the belief that they cannot forgive because they do not *feel* like it. But forgiveness is not an emotion. One can choose to forgive whether one feels like it or not. Many of us have had to reject our emotions, saying no to our natural inclinations, and firmly declare, "I forgive." Blessed is the person who can forgive!

Furthermore, in retrospect I realize that my mother may have been the victim of forces in her life that were beyond her control. I know nothing about her background. Perhaps she came from an unhappy home; for all I know she may have been rejected by her own parents. Rejection breeds rejection; those who have been abused as children often abuse their own children.

Of course, it need not be that way. I'm not suggesting that my mother was not responsible for what she did. But without Christ, without an understanding of her need for divine help, she was a victim of her own hatred, bitterness, and guilt.

People can be married and live in the same house without knowing the tensions that gnaw on their partner's soul. For all I know, my mother was going through her own private hell, a torment from which she knew no escape. Remembering that made it easier to forgive her.

Once a person has chosen to forgive those who have wronged him, the next step in emotional healing is praising God. The dean of women at a Bible college knocked on my door at a women's retreat. "Dorie, my mother didn't want me—no one loves me. Now I'm responsible for counseling 120 girls, yet I myself am bitter, lonely, and depressed." She continued telling me that she was overweight and didn't know how to overcome that problem.

When she was finished I assured her that I knew exactly

how she felt. After sharing her frustration with me, the depression which she had borne privately all those years began to dissipate. I suggested that we list all the good things God had done in her life. She shared how she had been chosen among many applicants to be the dean of women at her Bible school. She talked about God's goodness in giving her abilities and opportunities for ministry. Before she left I challenged her to make a list of all the good things God had given her, and then to thank God for each one.

The next morning I arrived at the auditorium for the final service of the retreat. To my delight they called upon the dean of women to sing. She prefaced her song with these words, "I've been at many women's retreats—but I always thought I knew what would be said. I'd heard it all before. The first night I stood at the door to listen; the second night I sat in the back row; and then last night I went to talk to our speaker. When I returned to my room I began to thank God for all the good things He has done in my life—the list was so long I stayed up for two hours talking to God and just praising Him. *This is the first time in three years I enjoyed getting up in the morning!*" Then she filled the auditorium with a moving song of God's love, a tribute to the Lord her God.

What this girl needed was a reminder that it is God's will that we thank Him for *all* things. "In every thing give thanks: for this is the will of God in Christ Jesus concerning you" (1 Thessalonians 5:18).

Our praise to God should not be dependent upon our feelings. We must consciously and deliberately learn to praise. A prescription for depression and bitterness is to read at least three psalms a day. Praise destroys gloom and dissipates depression.

Occasionally, adopted children have come to me. "Dorie, you at least knew who your mother was; you met your father. But I have to live with the knowledge that I was unwanted. My parents are out there somewhere, but I'll never even know who they are."

Whether it is more difficult never to have met your parents or to meet them and have them reject you, I cannot say. But I was an unwanted child, born when my mother was fifteen years old. I was probably the cause of her early marriage. But I have found comfort in the assurance that God has accepted me fully. God's gracious love is able to incorporate *any* person into His plan. The cross of Christ is the perfect remedy for the entangled messes of human misery. Christ anticipated all the ugly things of life—He foreknew the birth of all mankind and included everyone equally in His death. The question is whether we will respond to His love. In the Bible illegitimate children like Jephthah were used by God and became a part of His plan (Judges 11:1).

In the New Testament those who prided themselves in their natural origin were condemned by Christ. The Jews boasted that they were Abraham's descendants and were not born of fornication, implying that Christ was illegitimate (John 8:41). Christ was unimpressed with their lineage and accused them of being of their father the devil (v. 44). The fact that they knew who their earthly father was meant nothing; the issue was the identity of their spiritual father. I'm glad that if we are born into a human family that doesn't want us we can be reborn into a heavenly family that does!

Those who are born of "good stock" face the temptation of taking pride in their physical lineage. The result is that they do not see how desperately they need the grace of God. The Jews knew that their father was Abraham, and they rejected the Messiah. How much better if they, like the woman of Samaria, who was a half-breed, would have claimed no human merit but clung solely to Christ and His sacrificial work on the cross!

The Kingdom of heaven is populated with the downcast,

the helpless, and the unwanted. Those of us who cannot boast of our earthly lineage are special targets of God's love. As David wrote, "A father of the fatherless, and a judge of the widows, is God in his holy habitation" (Psalm 68:5).

To those who are struggling emotionally I cannot over-emphasize the need to read the Scriptures constantly, memorizing as many verses as possible. A child psychologist came to me after I had shared my testimony in a meeting and said, "Dorie, there isn't a reason in the world why you are not an emotional vegetable." Then she paused and added, "except for the grace of God."

How true! But that grace sustained me only because of my compulsive desire to find comfort daily in the Word of God.

In our home we say "I love you" all the time. Whenever we call or go out the door, we claim the opportunity to express our love. We enjoy planning surprises and giving small gifts just to say "I love you."

Once in New Guinea Burney ran in, crying, "Mommy, Mommy."

"What is it, honey?" I asked.

"Do you love me?"

"Burney, I love you more than anything," I answered as I squeezed him hard.

"That's OK," he answered breezily. "I just wanted to know." And back he went to his play.

In New Guinea we often played an "I love you" game. Lloyd would look at me and say, "I love you more than all the rocks from here to the river." Darlene would add, "I love you more than all the trees in Sentani." Someone else would say, "I love you more than all the stars in the sky."

Recently I received a letter from Darlene saying, "I love you more than all the mosquitos in Arkansas." Silly? I didn't think so!

I would never have survived life at Granny's house or my treatment at the Makins' or the painful rejection by my father and mother without the steadfast assurance of God's promises. To this day I have the New Testament Irma Fremm gave me with scores of verses I memorized underlined. The Word of God gives us the ability to cope with the aches and pains of our souls.

Some people have told me, "Dorie, you're not normal. Even children who have experienced far less rejection than you have hang-ups because of their background. Are you for real?"

My answer is that apparently God did an unusually deep work in my life, perhaps because I was so desperate. During my childhood I had virtually nowhere to turn; I had no shoulder to cry on. I threw myself at the Lord. Graciously, perhaps beyond what one might normally expect, He healed my crushed, embittered emotions. I'm convinced He can do the same for anyone who comes to God as I did.

My experience has also given me some tips to share with parents. Please tell your children you love them! In Chicago a man standing beside the casket of his fifteen-year-old son wrote a note and put it into the dead boy's hand. It read, "Son, I love you." How tragic to have waited until it was too late to say those words to a son! In our home we told our children we loved them; sometimes we told them several times a day. Today Burney and Darlene tell us, "Dad and Mom, we always knew you loved us, and we love you!"

Don't ever allow your dreams to take precedence over the careful rearing of your children. What could be more important than training them to live by biblical principles? It will mean pouring yourself into them to produce people honoring to God. That puts incredible responsibility upon us as parents. It means that we must take personal inventory of ourselves. What kind of person are *you?* That's the kind of person your child probably will become! We need God's help and wisdom with such an awesome task.

All the unfulfilled dreams in the world are not worth the investment of your life in one precious child. Of course it means sacrificing, putting aside some important goals to work toward a far more important goal—that of creating, loving, giving to, molding, and training your child to be a responsible person who loves and obeys God's Word. Your children will be living monuments to you, for good or for ill.

As much as Lloyd and I wanted to stay in the Baliem as missionaries, we felt it was wrong to force Burney to attend school away from home even though it was standard missionary policy. Yes, we were called to the Baliem, but we had to face the fact that first and foremost we were called to be parents.

My heart aches for the children of the United States. With the staggering divorce rate, a rise in child abuse, and the indifference of many parents, there are probably thousands of Doris Duckworths—unwanted, unloved, beaten, and neglected children.

To those brokenhearted children and bitter adults, I dedicate my life and ministry. To them I say, *What God has done for me, He can do for you.*

God can make us whole, if we give Him all the pieces.

21

Graveside Reflections

In 1972 we were driving through Kansas. "Honey, I
have a surprise for you—I'm going to take you to a special
place," Lloyd announced. Expectantly, I waited, unsure
of what he meant.

An hour later we approached a little town. "Dorie, look
at that name. Does it mean anything to you?"

"No— Wait a moment. Is this where my father was
born?"

"Yes."

We decided to try our luck at finding some information
about him or his family. We parked our car in front of the
corner store, walked in and asked, "Do you know someone
by the name of Duckworth—Lewis Duckworth?"

The man's mouth fell open. "Just wait a minute." He
went to the back of the store, and a moment later a woman
appeared. I was sure I was looking at a relative: the same
curly hair, dark eyes, dark skin.

"Did you know a Lewis Duckworth?" I asked, scarcely
believing my eyes.

"I'm a Duckworth," she answered, astonished. "Just a
minute," she said as she turned to call another man. He
walked to where we were standing. "Ask him what you
asked me," the woman ordered. When I repeated my question, he too was surprised.

"My mother raised Lewis Duckworth. She's ninety-five

years old—she was a Duckworth" the man told me. "Would you like to meet her?"

For a moment I thought I was dreaming. Nearly twenty-five years had passed since I had said good-bye to my father, and now I would meet the woman who had raised him! The woman standing before me was a distant cousin of mine.

We drove to the place where the man's mother was living. They brought her into the living room in a wheelchair. She was dressed in black, with white lace around her neck and wrists. I was told to kneel down since she was almost blind and could talk only in a whisper. Here was the woman who had raised my father.

"Mother, this is Lewis's daughter, Doris," the man spoke loudly.

"Honey," she motioned to me, "would you come closer so I can see you better?" The old woman ran her hand gently over my face.

"Your father was a good man. I'm sorry about what happened. Your family was Methodist—the shouting kind." She paused, a smile breaking over her wrinkled face. Then she gently put her hands on Burney and Darlene, "Oh, God bless you dears."

Again I looked into her eyes, and she put her arm around my neck. I kissed her cheek. My heart was bursting, longing to talk with her at length about my family roots. Her difficulty in speaking necessitated that our conversation be brief. "Someday," she whispered, 'I will tell you all about your father." That day never came; a few months later she died.

The man at the store asked me if I wanted to go to the cemetery. When we arrived the attendant opened the register, and we found this information: "Molly and Dell Duckworth died at the ages of 34 and 32 of tuberculosis."

"Doris," the man began, "these are your grandparents."

We walked down a narrow path until we came to a little graveyard. Two sunken graves with wooden crosses lay before us. There were the names "Molly Duckworth" and "Dell Duckworth." I stood motionless for several moments. Throughout my lifetime I had scarcely thought about having grandparents. Because of my mother's hatred for me, I had always suspected that someday a sordid story about my origin would come to light. And now for the first time I realized that I did have family roots—I did at one time have grandparents, although they died long before I was born. How I wished I could have met them! For all my ugly past, I was part of a family line.

Tears flooded my eyes. My children came to stand beside me. Darlene took my right hand, Burney my left. Then I heard the voice of God—the voice that had whispered to me during those many years of loneliness, sorrow, and heartache. *Dorie, your end is going to be so much better than your beginning.*

We turned to walk back to the car. My vision was blurred, my emotions churning. As we drove away, my thoughts shifted from the memories of my childhood to God's guidance in my life. Surely His grace is seen most clearly against a background of rejection and hopelessness. God had displayed His love to me in a hundred different ways. Yes, there was my mother, the orphanage, and my foster homes. Yet Christ had accepted me and elevated me to be an heir of God and a joint heir with Jesus Christ. He gave me a godly husband and two priceless children. Then He gave me the privilege of going halfway around the world to help stone-age people hear the gospel. And finally, He let me be a pastor's wife and tell others in America that God loves nobodies, and can make them into somebodies, for His name's sake.

He did all that for a girl nobody loved!

He raiseth up the poor out of the dust, and lifteth the needy out of the dunghill; that he may set him with princes, even with the princes of his people.

Psalm 113:7-8

Acknowledgement

We wish to thank Erwin and Rebecca Lutzer for the many hours of research and writing involved in telling this story. My husband and I appreciate Erwin's desire for accuracy and clarity in recording all of the details. His dear wife, Rebecca, typed and retyped the manuscript and provided the final editorial touches. Kay Oliver also spent many hours helping to finish the final draft. For all of this, Lloyd and I are deeply grateful. We are confident that God will use this story to show others the abiding power of the grace of God.

Doris and Lloyd Van Stone